in a
Pin-stripe Suit

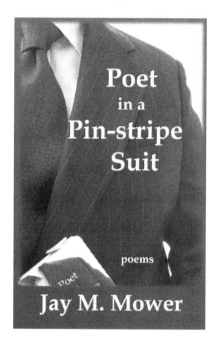

poems

Jay M. Mower

GARDEN OAK PRESS
Rainbow, California

Garden Oak Press
1953 Huffstatler St., Suite A
Rainbow, CA 92028
760 728-2088
gardenoakpress.com
gardenoakpress@gmail.com

First published by Garden Oak Press on June 15, 2020

ISBN-13: 978-1-7323753-8-3

Library of Congress Control Number: 2020935619

Printed in the United States of America

Contents

FOREWORD

Venturing into the forest of Jay Mower's poems is a literary exploration worth joining. As one who remembers Jay from a lifetime ago in Atlanta, and knowing something of the early ethos and cultural environment that surrounded him, I see again that along life's journey an individual may veer far from their early geographic sense of being and yet never so far as *not* to encompass all they have gathered along the way. Such is the Pindaric bounty discovered in the work of Jay Mower.

In these 10 sections, each one a poetic safari in itself, the reader begins to feel he or she is reading and listening to not one – but *Different Voices*, as one section is titled. In another, a different sound, as *The Swamp Witch* ". . .Rides the wind/ sings fire from her lips". . . then, in a complete turnabout – on the thundering hardwood of the *Roller Derby* – "Whippet Good *whips* Suzy Hotrod to outrace Em." Or, the more sadly humorous voice that's "got the Bipolar Blues." Then an elegiac one in *The Blue Dancer of Buenos Aires*, which "disappears with Eva, only beautiful lilies remain. . ."

The literary mind delves into different pasts and presents, depths and distances, or, in Jay's words, *Beyond Electricity* and *Strange Encounters, Visits to Dystopia*, then *Closer to Home* in an *Atlanta Spring*. And the pursuing reader, deep in the poetic landscape, encounters words, images and symbols transmuted into a language – so accurate, so revealing, so inexplicably true.

This literary treasure of Jay Mower's poetry is the real thing. In the opinion of this weathered observer, no poet writing today is more true to his personal vision – nor more eloquently expressive of its intrinsic values – than the author of this volume.

R. CARY BYNUM
Night Streetcars
Woodhall Stories
Reunion in Thera

for Family and Friends

Poet

in a

Pin-stripe Suit

poems

Jay M. Mower

GARDEN OAK PRESS

THE SWAMP WITCH

A promise made is a debt unpaid.

ROBERT W. SERVICE

At a New Orleans Bar

I can't believe they let him in,
washboard-weathered face,
piercing possum eyes and odor
of a polecat in heat.
Teetering on his bar stool,
the spent man offloads
his account of his night
with a mambo lady.

Man at Bar

Didn't know how black
her magic, deep the voodoo
vows, when she romanced me
with her brown jambalaya.
Couldn't have known she'd
cloak me in cypress honey,
but sure enjoyed her 'til she
shape-shifted and flew away.

Red Dress Redress

She sashays into the Cajun bar
encased in a skintight gossamer
red dress cheap as her thoughts
that enrobe me in a molasses
of lust. She blows in my ear,
a tickle that fuels our heat.
We sazerac to ecstasy, she extracts
a vow from my blood-starved brain
and with black moons in her eyes,
she shape-shifts and flits into
the quivering cypress sky.

On an unknown lawn, morning
dawns, I'm covered in cypress honey,
feel the power of gods coursing
my veins and discover pockets full
of lucre. I begin the life of Gatsby,
until one night, after a bender,
it's on my doorstep, my likeness
in miniature with a pin, piercing
the tiny heart, a penciled note
reminds of my unfulfilled vow.

I shudder in a cauldron of boiling
guilt and fear a looming train wreck
of troubles ahead, wonder whether
I will ever fit into God's sky
when the bayous empty into time.

The Swamp Witch

rides the wind, sings fire
from her lips and flakes
of ash rain over me.

I seek release from my vow,
a removal of the painful curse
on my skewered heart.

I rattle 'round root claws,
dodge overhanging bows
and flashes of my foolish vow.

She rests in her lair, deep
within the bayou where gators
guard and zombies look out.

When she rides the wind,
vents venom from her lips,
I avoid the skeeters, shun

cottonmouths and pray
her bad gumbo remains
in the rusted cast iron kettle.

Her Lair

Deep in the swamp beyond
where the mangroves grow,
I stumble into the washboard shack
where I seek to undo the voodoo.

Dark and fusty, a pentagram
centers the room, skull vases
surround a necromancer's globe
where she scries the pool
of departed souls between walls
that creep and crawl in a lizard
motif. Cobwebbed jars of newts,
embryos and pickled brains fill
nearby shelves. Zombie breathing
rasps pain into my ears, chills me,
but no visible beings appear.
I'm alone, except a black rose
beside a red-dress figurine,
glaring steel through my skin.

The Swamp Witch's Lament

Spanish moss teases my hair
under the press of cypress boughs.
Over the mucky soil, I glide
to my cabin, sense someone violates
this sacred space. Suddenly,
a man bolts out the door,
my own voodoo charm tucked
under his arm. I call my undead
who encircle the man who once
loved me, but left with his vow
empty as my zombies' brains.

He's trapped like a possum,
so I begin my magic chant,
when he needles my doll-knee
with a black pin of pure pain
and I must release his vow,
but he'll pay when I'm through.
Though above ground for now,
that man will wish he were below
each time the rooster crows,
yet a taint of acrid ash lingers
on my tormented tongue.

The Chase

I race past the root claws
and snake-filled bows, through
mud and muck with stolen swag,
but the steady tramp of dead feet
encircles and cuts me off.
I'm still and trembling.
She appears, demands her doll,
which I threaten with 13 black pins,
removed from a skull-jar in her lair.
Screeching as I jab one
into the knee, she agrees
to surrender my soul,
but extracts all my youth
and wealth, so you see
on this lonely bar stool,
what little is left of me.

THE TURTLE
AND
THE TIGRESS

Our breath is brief, and being so
Let's make our heaven here below.

ROBERT W. SERVICE

11

Man Splitting Mad

As arctic wind stabs like iron spikes,
his red and black checkerboard shirt
dances in the driven snow, while
his fury splits white oak logs.

He strikes hard, bright steel flashes
under the sun-bright blue sky. After
each axe stroke, surrounding firs
still to the silence he almost hears.

Whack. *Tigers mate with tigers,*
she leaves for some macho s.o.b.
Thwack. *Eagles soar, turtles plod,*
Suck-up Sam swipes my promotion.

Wrath seethes until his final blow,
at last the cord is cut. Warm now,
less need for the logs, chore done,
his anger's quelled, yet lives on.

Fissures in His Heart

The tigress gone, but lives on
in his despair. . .fair, flaxen hair
and red knit dress that hugs
her curved torso, knee to nape.

Every time he sees an iris, tastes
vanilla or smells bergamot,
amber Shalimar scent floods
her back into his senses.

He misses the hum of *Twilight Time*
any time of day and her gentle prod
to do more. Silence sounds
throughout his empty day.

Her touch soft as fallen snow,
yet warm as a hearth, evokes
a pang to fill a vacuum
far beyond his understanding.

He's frozen on an ice floe
of dreams, while anger shoots rays
through fissures into his heart,
not able to admit the reality of loss.

False Hope

The man grieves a new possibility
that soon flies further south
than the Galapagos, as he's
forced to cut another cord.

He gloated, Suck-up Sam – canned,
and now *he's the man*. Yet, not
a single tigress curl sparks when
he pleads love's renewed bond.

"Turtles don't grow feathers,
nor survive a busy highway,"
she smiles, adding he's bound by
the hard-wired paths that lead him.

Maybe his synapses short-circuit
like a hamster twirling on its wheel,
unable to escape ennui foretold
by his genes and the stars.

How can he avoid further disaster
and overcome his cruel master?

New Resolve

Today I will live in the moment, unless it is unpleasant,
in which case, I will eat a cookie. — Cookie Monster

Back at the woodpile, I whack at earlier
abandonment – Carolyn Smith rejected
my Valentine in grammar school. Whack,
friends let me down in the school election.

Only time mends a shattered self,
but who enjoys life's slowest days?
I can't heal through osmosis –
only axe whacks speed up time.
So I *unfriend* her on Facebook,
sign up for rage-based zumba
with an eye for fresh chicks, eat
Thai and watch *Downton Abbey*,
live spoon by spoon, unless
a particular sip sucks, then
I'll turn to rum-raisin Haagen Daz
and watch 220 *Three Stooges* episodes,
focus on my love of mountains,
climb to grace at a faster pace,
watch shooting stars, shoot pool
with buds and orbit Mars.

My future may be mysterious
to me, a rumor others don't see,
but I'll leave all that tattered baggage
at the threshold of yesteryear,
looking forward to one day when
I finally do myself a favor and make
the tigress an obscure footnote
in my history of chopping wood.

ROLLER DERBY

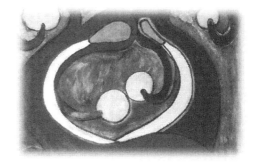

Friday Night Roller Derby

Oedipus Ref blasts his whistle, wheels roll.
Quad skates, helmets, pads, sports bras,
mouthpieces propelled by pseudonymous females –
Scald Eagle, Whippet Good, Peaches 'n Scream –
in Day-Glo *boutfits*, multiple tats on display,
race the oval, bumping and grinding to whip
a jammer past the pack to score. The tattoos
and tutus, piercings, fishnets, short shorts,
sundry garb adorn the Oaks Park crowd,
make me wonder if I've taken an irreparable
absence from my sanity.

Though feeling like the nerd primed for roasting
at a football banquet, I'm treated kindly,
ushered to prime seating beside a big roller mama.
Pierced concessionaires offer multiple smiles
and chances to win the half-time raffle,
while some Comic-Con characters respect
my space and woeful ignorance as I watch
toe dancing on skates, precisely timed bum bumping,
beaver cleavers and booty blocks in a sport
where offence, offense and defense are played
simultaneously. I become a *bleacher creature*.

The Zebras

Oft booed, razzed and jeered,
refs rule the rink – preserving
life, liberty and decorum.
They call you out for illegal blocks,
false entry and untimely starts.
Cutting the track and *falling large*
also activate the whistle as does
the ever-present fisticuffs.
Without the ref, bouts could be
an endless game of *Rollerball.*
Supreme Court on the floor,
all refs take abuse and more.
No wonder the camouflage –
stripes that moiré to make
the zebras harder to hit when
razz-berries and boos materialize.

The Pivot

Leader of the pack at first whistle,
the skillful pivot leads her troops,
manages her jammer through
the maze and retards enemy
jammer attempts to escape
the jumble of arms, torsos,
legs and skates in turmoil.
She arabesques to slam a rival
flat on the track or pirouettes
to a beaver cleaver, clearing the way
for her diva, the lead jammer,
to pass and score. Master
of the Velcro scrape
and fishnet burn, she enjoys
creating *waterfalls* and feasts
on fresh meat while earning
her roller name, I.M. Pain.

The Lead Jammer

Queen of the roller dome
during a jam, temporary
roller rink royalty, ballerina
on wheels, flat track diva,
hotrod honey, ruler of the oval,
fantasy of the opera, she ballets
through the air with the greatest
of grace. Her gilded quads,
winged like Mercury, glide
as she pirouettes the pack.
Her pointe work on skates,
C- and J- blocks galore, hip
checks control the floor.
She laps the pack
and the opposition jammer –
a *grand slam*, thank you ma'am.

Final Jam

The zebra inhales, exhales
Shrill whistle pierces the arena
    Quads rumble
    Blockers separate the skaters
        Two jammers spring forth
        split back of pack
    Scald Eagle *truck and trailers* Em-Dash
    through opposition blockers

but Whippet Good *whips*
Suzy Hotrod ahead to outrace Em
    Oedipus Ref whistles her
    lead jammer for the jam
        Suzy hot laps the oval, Em
        catches up, *C-blocks* Suzy
    over the padded rail and approaches
    pack back, ready to lap for a score

Number 2 blocker and pivot
snowplow in front of the pack
    opponents *fall small*
    like dominos on felt
        Em Dash passes, sees Suzy close
        behind, but knows win at hand
    decides to cash in on gain,
    hands on hips, stops the jam

Despite any joy of victory
or agony of defeat
    skaters roll on, knowing
    there's more than the score
        when you skate
        your wheels off

THE BLUE DANCER
OF BUENOS AIRES
& LOVE POEMS

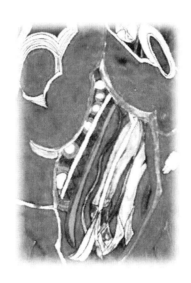

Blue Dancer of Buenos Aires

In my loneliness, I'll always have the Blue Tango.

— Amanda Lear

I see a wispy lunula
rise in the violet sky.
A slight wind whispers
through the window,
blows a blue dancer
out of the picture frame.

As she tangos,
my room becomes
a mass of dark and light blue,
red, yellow and orange rectangles,
like the houses of La Boca
covered with shipyard paint.

She palms my right back pocket,
wraps her fishnet stocking
coyly around my left leg.
Swaying to the lonely *Blue Tango*,
we move past buskers
on Calle Caminito to the front
of Bellas Artes al Aire Libre,
more a storefront than museum.

When you're leaving me – if I let you go
Take away my heart as I won't need it any more.

A cheap squeezebox barks
and strings alternate pizzicato and arco.
Musk seeps from her breasts
as she moves to the tango
and whispers in tempo:

I was loving you more than you will know
Cause I needed you, my darling. . .

Completely lost in the moment,
colorful houses of La Boca
are no longer visible,
vibrant papier maché sculpture,
yellow and red pottery disappears.
Murals show only a path to La Recoleta.

Remember how much I loved you
And let me go, like a Blue Tango.

She stands on the footpath
next to a stone tomb
and disappears with Eva,
only beautiful lilies remain.

Love Lost

She flies into a Vesuvian rage so quickly
I don't even recall what unleashed
the molten lava, but SLAM! SLAM! SLAM!
reverberates down the corridor
and an emptiness prisms hallway walls
from sunny to shades of lonesome blue.

Walking inside the darkening atrium,
I realize she's blazing bananas.
By the time I climb into my car,
I'm convinced she's *cucuzza* crazy.
My fantasy, *she'll soon be sorry.*

I toss her photo down the garbage chute
and mulch reappears. . .throw her name
into the recycling bin, but she comes back
as plastic wrap. Frantic, I mail her love
in a hate letter that returns postage due,
so I hurl her from Mount Quandary,
but she flows back as a gentle breeze.

Alone in myself, I miss gentle strokes
of her hand, the radiance of her laugh
and a wisp of her *Chanel.* She chases me
down the avenues, pulls me back
with gentle tugs and slithers into my mind
whether I'm gaming, preparing bids
or savoring backyard barbecued ribs.

TV tray after TV tray of silence penetrates
my mares-nest mind, loneliness screams
that her love will not return to me
on a simple spin of fortune's whim.

Altered State

Michelangelo's *David* wisps in smoke
da Vinci's *Mona Lisa* vacates her frame
Georgia O'Keeffe's calla lilies zephyr
Gershwin's Rockies and Gibraltar
tumble and crumble, the Nile evaporates
in little dust devils while the Sahara rises
to cirrus clouds, Beethoven's *Fifth*
titillates stone ears, only mutes pronounce
English properly, iron eyes watch
the Vargas Brothers Circus, Emily Post's
Etiquette vanishes to undisclosed locations
in the Library of Congress, ink from
our Bill of Rights melts off the page, stars
and stripes abandon Old Glory. I am lost
in a *Mad Max* world, in Tom Hobbes'
nasty, brutish, short life and you're gone.

Bending Reality

I love the word nelipot, and it has a solid etymology
from the Greek for "barefoot."

— Other-Wordly *website*

Tired of goofy words, my iPad nods off. I pass
kaleidoscope oils that pop off white studio walls
and nelipot down a spiral staircase where
brown, yellow, red, black and white men,
dressed in stark penguin attire, chauffeur
multi-hued taffeta and chiffon across parquet
under crystal chandeliers to a big band beat
conducted by Glen Miller's phantasmal baton.

I muster enough *chutzpah* to tango
with a *Dior-draped* dish languishing
on the sidelines. She ignores my odd attire
and performs majestically, scenting
my senses with *Chanel,* as we summon
stares from dancers and musicians alike.
Yet, the beat continues until I feel a tap
on my left shoulder and a lavish

Veronica Lake-blonde cuts in, airs
her *Lancôme* fragrance and completes
our folk ballet with a horizontal dip.
Chest to breast, cheek to cheek, we linger
and I yearn for more as the chandelier dims
and we drift into a land of rainbows.
The vanilla with patchouli deep notes,
orange taste of fuchsia lips, supple fabric

of her skin and warmth of her heartbeat
pounding my torso, vanquish all inhibitions.
Her tresses flow as she melts below
in my arms and reality's bent beyond
human recognition, then I sense feelings
temporal as that waft of *Lancôme* vanishes.
She fades supine into the parquet while
I float above to the rainbow chandelier.

Taste of Coconut Cake

Eyes flutter, I'm completely uncovered. Dipping
into a dreamscape, my shaky ego tiptoes
like red balloons in a cage of spooked porcupines.
I'm frozen in *what might have been*, a familiar time loop.

The highway from Portsmouth Navy Yard narrows
to a dot in my rear-view mirror then closes
when York village looms on the right. Foes, fiends
and friends chip away my mask, so I risk exposure
at the front porch of your white frame house.
Tomorrow I'm off to ports unknown and you're
on the road to study unexplored Italy,
fish-hooked by your parents to follow a path
while I'm still seeking one. My resolve falters
like slain umbrellas in a wintry Chicago wind
and I don't want to face humiliation.
In that era before *Facebook* friend, *Twitter* tweet
and *Skype* encounter, I don't *pop the question*
and risk your rejection. We just agree to *keep in touch.*

Though I know the taste of coconut cake
without studying the stars or Immanuel Kant,
I should have known the wind can't speak
or whistle thoughts across the sea.
Lost in this empty bed 50 years later,
I still feel your song wafting away.

Of Popcorn and Conversation

Rhett ends the conversation frankly
not giving a damn, Scarlett falters
at his abrupt manner, reels away
from the Tiffany-windowed door,
swoons on the plush of maroon stairs,
looks up and emotes her *mañana* lines.

Scarlett *fiddle de dees* tomorrow, always
hungering for her lost man, meal or manor.
I'm not as able – when careless with words
tender as dew on a rosebud, my squeeze
takes simple words further south
than Tara before my next heartbeat.

Under a canopy of stars, crickets singing,
she cuddles beside, blinks and smiles,
"We should get married." An answer
tomorrow won't work, yet I could be
swept away in a scarlet firestorm
or inundated in torrents of tears.

Everything Changes

The summer field, sun-fed, mutable.
— Ellen Bryant Voigt

The poet wrote, summer fields change,
yet scientists tell us not only summer,
but also winter, spring and fall are
variable, just like the densest objects
in our universe, neutron stars. Even
the heaviest elements, osmium, mercury
and basalt wriggle internally. In creation,
particles constantly fluctuate up, down,
in, out, back and forth, ever so slightly,
nothing lasts, naught is still. . . So
after the pans fly and plates cry,
she comes to me, all pouty faced,
says, "You don't love me anymore."
My reply. . . *All is mutable.*

Take Five

Our history
Yearning, hesitating
You pass by, I'm not able to speak
Brubeck

As you glide to the dance floor once more,
I see that almost smile I can't read, yet
the mystery of your Mona Lisa *maybe*
warms my room to springtime as our eyes
touch for just a moment. The drummer beats
a slow jazz rhythm in rare 5/4 time,
the piano and bass weave a carpet,
then the alto with its blue melody,
scales the walls, crests and rolls back down
only to soar once more. Yet each time,
my frozen tongue fails, unable to say
what both of our hearts long to hear.
You're Carmen McRae singing *what could be*
as Dave's quartet harmonizes, but I'm
the yearning boy from Ipanema,
lost in a different song.

That Hamburger

Finger-picked lettuce
creamy avocado just off
a glossy-leafed tree
hand-plucked ripe
round red tomato
bacon crisped in the pan
cheddar from Tillamook
mayo slathered from a jar
pickles dilled by Heinz
and crème-de-la-crème
virtually fat-free ground
beef grilled to perfection
stacked Babel tower high
on a Kaiser bun bought
fresh from the corner bakery
a burger meant to be
savored in leisure but
such culinary joy was
consumed in a single gulp.

Macy's men's department
one hour later a pang
crescendos into a slow
rumble at my belt that
erupts into a belly-bending
jolt bringing sweat beads
to brow and tremors
throughout the body
while blood escapes
my brain until I pass from
consciousness floor-flat
concerned clerks circling
over me – yet far easier
this painful indignity
than the vacant hallways
Chanel-deprived sheets
and silent scullery
of my lonesome abode
that accompanies the
everlasting loss of her
warmth by my side.

Aqua Pura

From the foothills, Italian Alps ahead,
Lombardy behind, virgin snow, infused
with minerals and sparkling, filtered
through dolomitic peaks a quarter mile
above the sea, surfaces from a 30-year
underground journey to tease the tongue
and tang the nose as San Pellegrino pours
from the green *Vichy* bottle with four pale blue labels
and a single red star into my narrow-rimmed crystal.

I add a blood orange freshly plucked from the tree
in our yard and sliced into succulent quarters
to tame a slight bitterness and allow the fine bubbles
in this glass of delight tingle my nose, freshen
my mouth and summon a yearning to ride bikes
over the top of Lucca's walls, re-hike thousands
of footfalls up and down the Cinque Terre and
see your smile that douses all but a tinge of heartache.

That Old Black Magic

Louis and Keely's vocal ends
followed by a bumblebee buzz
on the sax while my last sip
of scotch whiskey disappears
off the rocks. Halloween and Keely,
I'm drawn to magic spells, witches
and a spider that spins elastic
catenaries, no visible knots,
glistening across the morning
sidewalk to a weatherworn fence,
like the web you once wove
when you kissed and lured me in
and we vibrated in a magic dimension
to the old Southern Pacific
as it rumbled past your apartment.

Joie de Vivre

Perhaps you know that I've gone
through life searching for you.
from the lyrics of Buscándote

Music moans musk, a *bandoneon*
tangos lust while on the terrace
an amber moon silhouettes dancers
moving in step to *Buscándote* rhythms
wafting through the louvers. Champagne,
lovers and their beautiful women
perfume the ballroom when she appears
like Venus to end my search forever.

She accepts my command, we glide
across the floor into white clouds
over the pampas. We float as one,
our bodies silently dialog through swivels
and thrusts of passion not understood,
only experienced in rippling rivers
of the twilit sky. Her leg flows from the slit
in her sequined silver shift. We interlace
and as I spin, this vertical tête-à-tête
becomes our horizontal wish at the moment
a *bandoneon* barks its final fading chord.

The Red Dress

Ohmamaohpapa, Baby, Baby!

I'm gone when you slip that red dress on.
No buzz from martinis compares
with the tingle in these admiring eyes.
Gossamer, sleeveless, strapless –
confess, I want to walk you through
all venues known and let all the men
envy your charm and my good fortune
to stroll with you on my arm. Yet, I
dream of going to that room far from
where your mother and father are,
so I no longer have to guess what's
beneath that flowing red dress.

Wistful Love

Yesterday is dead and gone
and tomorrow's out of sight.
— Kris Kristofferson

Rain sheets my windowpane.
A distance wordless call whispers,
cries *never too late*, yet here I wait
for a sign to prod me to what I deny.

Though I was born too soon for any
encounter to bloom, she captivates
my mind when we meet over dogs,
furry ones, at the neighborhood park.

Perky shape, blondish hair
and an enchanting beam halos her,
sure, she's made several spins
around the sun, but gentle ones.

Though I cannot tell how words began,
yet magnetic waves pulsed through me.
We talk of dogs, children and mention
significant others to show *no hit intended*.

When she did suggest we meet,
walk the canyon together,
I brighten, even though I know
the relationship cannot grow.

As the rain sheets this window, my pain
realizes how important to enjoy
the present moment, hope for more
and not telescope a future that cannot be.

Regrets

homage to William Carlos Williams

That one night
we shared
your tapioca,
snug as furry slippers

I vowed
to drive you
to the station
with my pick-up

Though the tapioca
was warm, sweet,
delicious, the Navy
sirens beckoned

Amour

1. 1917 Portland

Woodrow Wilson inspires him
to fight in the war to end all wars.
Too young to serve, my father
lies about his age, joins the AEF,
is shipped overseas.
Disillusioned by the inscription
Gott mit uns in the dead German's helmet,
he lies on the ground, freezing
alone in the black and white
battlefields of 1918 France,
stomach knotted by foul water,
contaminated reserve ration,
rancid bacon and hardtack;
bowels spewing foul smelling
bloody cysts and mucus.
After the owl whispers,
he sees his mother's broad face.
She's wearing her black kitchen dress,
white apron, hair knotted in a bun.
He feels warmth of bread baking
in the hearth stove as a Maine
winter whistles outside.
He hears tears in her deep alto voice
as she says: *Get up so I won't be disappointed.*

2. *1974 Atlanta*

I hold my mother's hand,
gossamer living room curtains are drawn.
We sit on a taupe tweed sofa
facing my father who is supported
by two pillows on a black
Naugahyde recliner.
He's fed by tube; body wasting away,
skin cells attacking skin cells,
jaw so eaten, his face looks like leftovers
from a butcher's block.
My vision blurs when Mother
asks how he can be so cheerful.
He struggles, little left, whispers:
That's the least I can do with all the suffering
you must go through.

DIFFERENT VOICES

Different Voices

We place people
in little boxes
behind labels: depressive,
schizoaffective, bipolar,
James, Jill and Jane look out
in their Arctic isolation.

Odd and quiet at a cocktail party,
eccentric James crosses the Styx
and falls into deep depression.
Interesting Jill's logic wanders
back and forth like the Mississippi
as her ideas and risky affairs
alarm the Mensa convention.
Spontaneous Jane risks freedom
with dangerously unpredictable
fingering in shark-infested waters
roiling at the Lord & Taylor
Contemporary Shop.

Is it still James, Jill or Jane
behind the mask?

I've Got the Bipolar Blues

My ego done told me,
life's so good and grand,
I oughta travel first class
every time that I can,
buy a new Caddy, black and red
and a big château with a feather bed.
Wanna capture all the rush,
goina spend 'til I'm out on my tush.

My checkbook done told me,
after goin' from black to red,
all my yesterdays
were the best of days,
after standing so tall,
now I'm teetering to fall
wanna pump some lead
into my sorry old head.

I've got the bipolar blues
I've got the bipolar blues
Yeah, yeah, I got the bipolar blues

My doctor done told me,
mood swings ain't no cause
for alarm once a little lithium
and Effexor work their charm,
but then, my body done told me
all these pharmas and crap
are putting a serious crimp
on my life in the sack.

I've got the bipolar blues
I've got the bipolar blues
Yeah, yeah, it's no wonder
I've got these low-down,
low-low-down bipolar blues.

On the Way Back to San Diego

fatigued and famished, my wife finds
an Italian restaurant listed in Las Vegas.
We can't find the Capri Ristorante
until we realize it's inside the casino
at Sunset Station. I'm thinking
Dante's inscription on the gate of Hell:
Abandon hope all ye who enter here.
When I hesitate, our granddaughter pules:
I'm hungry, so the wife nods and we enter.

The bulletproof glass door slides
open to a smoke-filled ambiance
thick as the morning coastal layer
with red, yellow, blue, green neons
peeking through. I smell
cheap patchouli and feel a sting
like iodine in my eyes.
Characters from the *Star Wars*
bar scene mingle, some stand,
others astride red scooters
or plopped on deep-red plastic stools.
Some have green portable oxygen tanks.
With all the arms, hands, wrists
and fingers in perpetual motion, seems
like we're at a Gold's gym with disco lights,
but this looks like a lot more fun
and who knows, Fortuna
just might smile on me tonight.

I'm thinking: *Why not?*
but as I slow, the eight year old
singsongs: *I can't wait to tell Mommy.*

Word Salad

When the message is "cna you raed this"
or the sign reads "solw" or **"sotp"**
th esen ten ces eem sto hav est ran ges pac ing,
you may be an Einstein or Cher.

If you're looking through a fish eye,
the page swirls like Charybidis
and you feel like the rock,
you may be an Agatha Christie or daVinci.

If the margins fade like an Arizona sunset,
       y Isl
      e   a   ler
    n   n l c ter
   o   d ro oas r
lines are C   ides. . .
and reading is like being sick at sea,
you may be an Edison or Walt Disney.

If the p rotates to q and the d backflips to b
t decides it no longer needs a crossbar
and i neglects to wear its cap or looks like j
e gets lazy and drops its – to become c,
who knows how great you can be.

Anosognosia

When her daughter enlightens her:
Seashells are man's creation
fashioned from primal clay
made by hand
to serve as currency
from time immemorial,
she wonders if she's honoring
her daughter, the devil or herself
when she sees no danger, no harm
and does not rise to the bait,
does not pick up the rope,
does not disagree, but seeks
a mutually accepted reality.
"That may be, dear, but as you know,
scientists and creationists have
differing opinions, too. Sit down.
Could I fix you some tea?"

The Coin

*Minds that have withered into psychosis are
far more terrifying than any character of fiction.*
— Christian Baloga

A quarter by the parking meter
winks at me and begs for a home.

As I bend to pick it up, I plummet
into Charybdis. Glass eyes peer
through my skull, doorway shadows
whisper menace, fear-sweat stench pervades.

*The voices rage and flow, at first
 pianissimo and then they grow.*

Hisses from the alley breed maelstroms
out of a calm sea, mixing memory with desire,
stirring dry kindle into a stormy harvest,
crushing hope and peace in arctic floes.

*My thoughts ebb and flow
like nothing you'd care to know.*

Jesus is watching, waiting,
keeping score. Will I be tried
on Urantia for indiscretion?
Why single me out? What next?

The aura of blue uniforms and white frocks
controls the street. Where's my knife?
Strangers circle, whisper, judge me.
I'm ordered to stand still, say no more.

*The white gowns come and go
smelling of Mop & Glo.*

I feel restraints on wrist and leg,
console eyes pierce my skin,
Twilight Zone music controls
my synapses. I smell anesthesia.

Were Life a Keyboard

I'd use *control* as desired
option if that didn't work
function when in a fog
select *shift* for emphasis
return when desired
delete when too painful
but never *escape*.

The Therapist

Though I have as much money
as turtles have feathers,
I need a good therapist
or someone to listen to my drivel
with a completely open mind,
someone who'll appreciate
my poems, never disagree
with my motives, always agree
with my opinions and never judge
my actions, or me, even when wrong,
but money doesn't deter me,
I'm headed straight for the pound.

The Edge

Contentment is natural wealth,
luxury is artificial poverty.

— Socrates

Darkness comes early today.

A shrouded sun silhouettes
concrete pillars, frozen in a row,
shivering as an icy Gotham wind
whistles the avenue.

As ants scurry the pavement
50 floors below, an empty suit
contemplates the edge
and the poverty of plenty:

I remember the joy of sunrise
when my Armani was previously owned,
my Jaguar, a beetle and the penthouse,
a five-flight walk-up; a banquet
was Chinese take-out in white cartons,
the symphony, a solo in the shower
my portfolio, a dream and awards
glistened in the smiles of friends.

World Suicide Prevention Day

September 10th

A parent reflects

What can I expect today?
Sometimes I know.
There's the manic high
Grandiosity, religiosity,
Then the slide into darkness,
Despair, depression and the abyss.

Sometimes not.
All seems normal
Calm day, pleasant dinner
Good night, Mom
Good night, Dad.

Sometimes it's a real effort.
Thought out
Carefully planned
Seriously executed
With no lifeline.

Other times, not.
It's thought out
But just one pill too few,
Seat belt on, horizontal slashes
And the lifeline was there.

Sometimes, success.
All you can do is grieve
And move on.
Sometimes, not –
and there is still hope.

When She's Florence Nightingale

smells of warm apple, cinnamon
and nutmeg waft through the house.
When she's Florence,
you would eat off the floor,
puzzles get solved,
laughter fills the room
and altar brass gleams
with a sparkle of devotion.
When she's not, shadows creep
from the crevices of doom.
She's diarrhea city, shrunken
to less than 87 pounds,
doubting more than Saint Thomas
and – Jove, take cover – when she leaves
the darkened corners of her dungeon.
As I sit here in outplacement,
waterboarding my mind,
the jobs I want I cannot get
the jobs I get I do not want,
I remember one of those dark days
when I left for Cambridge
and she shared her darkness,
". . .and if you don't make it,
come home, don't kill yourself."

A counselor reminds me, "Stop being
Sisyphus, repeating and expecting
different results – Einstein's
definition of insanity." I realize
a need for change. At the company,
I got my allowance every two weeks,
did my chore list and didn't fight
with my brothers and sisters.
Fireworks in my head tell me
it's time to bake apple pie,
clean up the mess
and restock the larder.

Mary Jane, I Love You

You're my best friend,
you know how to soothe me
when I'm riled and make
tough times better.
You know just what I need,
make me one mellow fellow,
and my work sensational.
Mary Jane, how can I help
but love you?

Oh, those terrible things they say.
How could it be? You're no Jezebel.
You're so good to me now,
you'd never turn on me,
would you?

The 38ᵗʰ Parallel

Full of energy, he signs up
for 15 credit hours, drops
to 12, six, three and now
he's upstairs in his room.

He agrees to see a psychiatrist,
take his meds, work towards
recovery, then forgets, and now
he's upstairs in his room.

He agrees to find a job, washes dishes
for a week, quits, serves burgers
for two, is axed and now
he's upstairs in his room.

He agrees to do volunteer work
at the pound, 10 hours per week,
pressure's too great, and now
he's upstairs in his room.

He agrees to clean up after meals,
take out the garbage, keep his room neat,
he forgets, struggles, stews and now
he's upstairs in his room.

I don't want to become Geppetto.
Let my son be Pinocchio,
free to fight battles, flail and fail
or triumph without my strings,

yet, where is that 38ᵗʰ parallel, a place
where illness begins, manipulation ends?
Seems a moving target and I'm caught
in *Catch 22*, not knowing what to do.

Depression

I'm so worthless,
don't even bother to listen.
I have as much value as pond scum.
Every day is just more of the same
dreariness, ennui, loneliness.
Nothing is worth doing,
seeing, hearing, smelling
tasting or feeling.
(I wish I could feel something.)
The night is black, so is the day.

Weeping Jacaranda

The jacaranda sheds lavender tears
on the playground while a grieving mother
cries silent tears at the station, remembering
the promise of spring blossoms, the bitterness
of lost years and the wintry irons around his wrists.

Who Says This Can't Be Love?

I can ease your every fear
better than anyone. When you
don't get the prize, I ache
from your every pain.

I'll take off a day at work,
forego an afternoon with friends
and miss a wonderful party,
just to be with you.

I'll always say yes,
no matter what you ask
and be there for you,
no matter how often you lie.

I'll wash your socks,
trim your toenails,
hold my tongue, bottle anger,
buy you that smart phone.

I'll make the ultimate sacrifice
as Juliet did after Romeo,
just to keep the embers
of our love glowing.

I live only for your smiles,
nothing more.
Why can't others see
this has to be true love.

Boundaries

When he calls me *Bitch, Cunt, Whore,*
he's banished to sleep in the garage.
When he pokes a hole in the wall
or tosses dishes around the kitchen,
he's off the property, but can return
when he can control himself the next day.
When he raises his fists, hits me
or threatens to snuff his life
and my fear swells oceanic,
I punch 911 and to get help.
These are stopgaps until that day
I can say, "Paul, straighten your room
and we'll go for pizza" or "Paul,
take out the trash and I'll bake cookies,"
and hope for even more.

First Visit

No belt, jeans drape below his hips,
hair spews in Lady Liberty spikes,
no shoe laces, attendants as guides,
he drags his lumbering body
through dense fog, out of a sterile cell.
Others in psych lock-up stand around
with the blank stare of a glass-eyed doll
as he shuffles over to face us,
almost no expression or sign of life
crossing his pale face when he gazes
through his mother as if she were a window.
Silence stills the room.

Frustration

Although he's 23
his hallway has no doors
his piano plays off-key
his lift serves no floors

When he decides to go
his lorry has no wheels
his bakery has no dough
his diner serves no meals

He ignores all escapes
gives danger not a thought
his salad has no grapes
his movie has no plot

Though on quixotic quest
like Ahab after whale
his mom hesitates to suggest
his train will derail

She hopes he'll come to see
his odometer is so blank
he's lost in Tennessee
with only himself to thank

She prays that some fine night
though his hallway has no doors
he'll recognize his plight
and get the help he abhors

Visit to Boston

My daughter and I
go to Boston to see
her nephew, my first
grandson. Words slice
like a razor when
my son corners me,
> *Please keep my sister*
> *in tow around little Bob,*
we aren't sure how
she will behave after
> *all those weeks*
> *in the psych lock-up.*
Though she's never been violent,
even in her wildest psychosis,
I know no words will change
the fear I see in my son's eyes
or hear in his voice, so I absorb
a blow below the belt,
silently hover like a Black Hawk
on a mission to protect her ego,
to protect him from his fears
and little Bob from god knows what.

Catalyst

A young man sleepwalking
through a peasouper
along the Yangtze
doesn't speak Chinese.

His father casts a beacon
the son cannot see,
shouts directions
he cannot hear,
throws a rope
he cannot grasp,
grills a prime sirloin he can
neither smell nor taste.

His father seeds clouds
with silver iodide,
stands by his side,
waits for a clearing rain.

The Dream

Honors in Stockholm,
the red carpet in Oslo,
MacArthur award or a Pulitzer,
Washington office at One First Street,
or a bed at 1600 Pennsylvania Avenue.

School a breeze, no obstacles seen,
your ideal teen, then fog descends.

FBI channels thoughts,
outer space visitors establish
his deity; he must save sinners.
His thoughts appear front page
The New York Times,
Chuck Barris recruits him
for the CIA.

Still atop the world,
he prophesizes,
crashes the barriers,
speaks with seraphs,
commandeers merchandise,
finds himself chained
in a bottomless chasm.

Gradually the fog dissipates.
A phoenix, he learns to create
and accept new destinations
where palms sway
in the gentle breeze
of a lush tropical isle,
and there is shelter from storms.

DEAR CLEMENTIA
&
OTHER PERSONS OF NOTE

Dear Clementia

homage to Traci Brimhall

Fat and ugly as you are,
HPV and all, Harry Tischler
would have been killed first.
Fat hunkering ox calf,
almond wallpaper complexion,
horn rims perching on toucan beak,
black marbles under dark wool,
our wolf pack pummeled Harry
daily because he was a Jew,
one of the Jesus-killers
on page 212
of Mrs. Jones' bible stories.
East Lake schoolyard was his Dachau.
Those of us who did not bare our teeth
held books for those who did.
Years later, I see his doppelgangers
in a mass burial projected on ivied walls
and the wounds caused by holding books
became incarnate. Holocaust museums
in Washington, Houston, Berlin, Budapest
reinforce the cost of being a lemming.
Harry's pain sowed subterranean seeds
for the six short weeks he tolerated
fifth grade, so I could grieve a battered
Matthew Shepard tied to a fence post,
James Byrd dragged three and a half miles
over asphalt behind a rusty pick-up,
Emmett Till dumped in the Tallahatchie
with a ceiling fan bijoux
and a barbed wire neck chain.

Harry has the looks, experience
and credentials to be your partner,
the god of forgiveness. If he agrees
Hitler loves Jews, paraplegics tap dance
and Harry is an *übermensch.*

Sylvia and Andrea

To err is human; to forgive divine.
— Alexander Pope, *An Essay on Criticism*

One June night as a blue moon shines
through the diaphanous, a shadow
crashes the barriers into her mind
and silent words leap from the page.
Her soundless cry screams
the pain of Rachel weeping
for her children, but Sylvia's poem
plans filicide like Medea, then
a week later, she shifts to suicide.

What Sylvia left unfulfilled
a half-century ago, her poem
portends on that June day 2001,
when Andrea draws fatal water
to the porcelain bathtub ring,
baptizes her quiverful of five
into the mystery beyond life.

No doubt, Andrea knew Satan
clutched their little hearts and
was certain they went to heaven.
Yet, her certitude thrusts me
into a kaleidoscope of doubt,
can humans recycle, does god
hover above in dark matter,
reside inside man or exist at all
when men justify war and murder?
At least that old moon shining
gossamer has nothing to ponder,
to be sad about.

Ahab Remembered

Where we choose to be – we have
the power to determine that in our lives.
— Sena Jeter Naslund, *Ahab's Wife*

Neither my first nor last husband,
he was the most heroic and not mad.
How would you feel if your leg went
like a shaft of wheat in the reaper?

Though older, pretty decent
between the sheets; witness
our strapping son Jehoram.
I like the smell of sea salts
and loved the old whalebone.
Progressive thinker,
he spoke up for me in public
when I was criticized
as a cotton-picking Abolitionist,
even agreed I should pleasure
with the porcelain cucumber
while he's away after prey.

Don't understand all this fuss
about a fish, but how can you
not see his bravery,
lashed to that white whale,
resolute to his final thrust,
like the gold doubloon
he affixed to the mast
of the *Pequod*?

Edith's Untold Story

a fresh take on an Old Testament tale

Regardless what modern poets write,
must admit peeking back was a mistake.
Unlike George Bailey, no angel Clarence
flapped down to alter my history. I've rued
that moment for over 4,000 blue moons
that've circled overhead, especially
when I wasn't around to protect
my virgin daughters.

It makes no difference
whether I was disobedient,
slipped on a lump of halite,
became a curious monkey,
longed for one last glance
at abandoned friends and family,
was angry with God because
He spoiled the Sunday bridge party
and broiled our homestead
or if I just wasn't paying attention.

I stand, a pillar of salt overlooking
the Dead Sea, oxen at my feet
licking my toes every morning
while righteous Lot, who was
so chummy with angels while I sorted
laundry, changed diapers, wiped noses,
kept a kosher kitchen in a heathen land
(no easy task), got a pass. Wasn't me
who offered our daughters for sex
with Sodomites, who'd then get stoned,
bonk Becky one night and her younger sister
the next, yet I'm the one standing here.

Damn right, I have regrets, should
never have married the righteous bastard
to begin with, wouldn't have moved
to Sodom, had daughters turned to sluts
and these dumb-oxen at my feet.

Thoreau's Dream

While other men busy about their beans,
I avoid the poverty of plenty
and chains of conformity,
enjoy the true wealth of nature,
spend my life lavishly
in sunrises and rainbows.

I dream of times when armed forces
can no longer stage a decent parade,
when the business of politics
is building roads, schools
and bridges to community,
the helm of industry steers
toward service to mankind
and the meaning of life shimmers
in the ripples of a pond.

Wrested, Raked and Riffled

A vibrant Latin voice judders, entreats me
to hear how wrested from the quarry
and violated. Amazons kneel conquered
and subjected at every corner, Roman men
dominate her façade, spring forth larger
than their horse-mounted prey, slash limbs away,
decapitate numerous warriors. Her beauty
bewildering, but emblazoned on casket sides,
these reminders, history is carved by the victors.

Though her master was accomplished,
she struggles to express depths of her pain.
Of all museum-goers, she chooses me.

Goes on to describe her cuts by pitching,
rough stabs at the point of chisel and hammer,
refinement at the scrape of rakes and rifflers
over myriad months, followed by sand
and polish over her entire calcite corpse.

Worse than the pain, the shame
of how they violated her exterior
with an embellished memorial
to a male chauvinist, filled her chest
with his ashes and punched incense holes
in her extremities to honor the pig.

Pauses, then sobs about leaving
the quarry where she was recognized
as a natural beauty, sad that her life
preceded Michelangelo. In the right hands,
would have tolerated the pain gladly,
if only to become a David, Moses or the Pieta,
instead she endured long years
with an incomplete soul inside,
the remains of a so-called Roman hero.

Dozing Through
the French Revolution

I shall seize fate by the throat.
— Ludwig von Beethoven

While the gang tipples at Cronin's
off the Square, paper due, I'm trying
to make sense of the French Revolution,
fighting a cauldron of ennui and sleepiness.

Burke's *Reflections*, Doyle and Carlyle
histories succeed as anesthesia, I hear
the three individual quarter notes in G
then E-flat for two beats on 89.7,

some say fate knocking at the door, others
liberté, égalité, fraternité.
Blood cleanses Place de la Concorde,
Republican ideals knock at each Parisian door,

the over-taxed shopkeeper, tinsmith and baker,
refuse to watch the nobles eat cake,
fund wars and dance money away,
they rise, take to the Paris boulevards.

Peasants rebel at the pursuit of hare and hart
trampling their crops, workers at the want
of bread, the entire third estate at servitude
and tithes to a Church amassing land beyond need.

I hear the sound of blood on Parisian streets,
record tri-color red, white and blue flags
that wave at gatherings. The fury persists
because the gods are sanguine in my masterwork.

Extra trombones, contrabassoon and piccolo
aid my journey through conflict to victory.
Dissonance, *vivace* and *allegro* scream through my work
so no one can sleep, yet I awaken to a blank page.

Monet at Giverny

Because of flowers. . .I've become a painter.
— Claude Monet

As silent flora scream for immortality
I blaze my brush across canvas
capture a cacophony of color
compose a floral symphony

Iris and tulips carry the theme
wisteria and dahlia flourishes add variation
as my baton transforms chaos to music
freezes a rhapsody of delight

Colorful melody echoes the pond
water lilies clap to tempo
and bamboo sways
reverberating our joy

Coming Home

homage to Robert Frost

He enjoys chill darkness, no shadows as strands
of black capellini sparkle rime on tarmac.

His life roils like a sackful of mallets, his quest,
a backpack full of snakes and pockets of potential.

The dead lurk in his dreams, become white tigers
harrying him to dawn before he turns and chases them.

With memories churning in empty rooms,
he looks backward with pride, forward with hope.

In clandestine lands with flowers thick like mist,
he perceives a thousand people with one face.

Troubled when two opposite things are true,
he's consoled by warm thoughts of home.

When you return to the hearth in frost, they must
take you in, even with a shadow over your breath.

Power of Smoke and Grease

homage to Philip Levine

Baptisms in brine of car parts,
dead fish and broken bikes,
ceilings fall in long bandages,
we pound sand in the charred
remains of our soil, toil
and sweat with hands emptied.

Stark black and white photos,
autos from River Rouge or mom's
apple pie, life's glass never
overflows, no thing's worth more
than any one of us, yet the earth
spins at its own sweet will.

His poems in black and white,
stories and confessed lies,
will haunt paper, screens, air
and skies, until I'm able
to calculate the value of pi,
now a dark Caddy's his ride.

Dante's Advice for Young Princes

Obvious as a lion
tending herds of gnus,
some tongues wag slander,
the bold resort to assassination
and the devious ostracize.

Instead, I mix oak galls, wine
and vinegar, quill
venom over velum
while my ink horn
pumice stone and knife
rest at my side, eternally
impugn names of men who
harm, sully or disparage me,
use media to show Charon
pole a punt of select souls
across the Styx. Burn corrupt clerics
in sand and rain, repay wrathful
Filippo's slap and lies as he gurgles
under foul water and flame heretic
Farinata in his fiery tomb.
Though still alive, I prepare
a filthy ditch for the simoniac
Pope Boniface VIII to circle
forever in leaden robes.

Modern times call for clever ways
to wrest power, but if you rule lands
of heathens, contact fellow Fiorentini,
Niccolò Machiavelli. Though younger
than I am, he has many excellent ideas
on how to prosper.   *Ciao*.

Adolph Eichmann

The sad truth is that most evil is done by people
who never make up their minds to be good or evil.
— Hannah Arendt

Regardless of what you hear
about the Final Solution, I'm proud
of my zeal in cleansing the Reich
of undesirables. Perhaps if I had
worked even more relentlessly,
the Mossad never would have
rousted me from my
Argentine pleasure palace.

Will admit how embarrassed
I am, a super mensch, caged
like an animal, out of uniform,
in a very plain gray V-neck,
rumpled slacks and comfortable
brown shoes while my inferiors
render their final judgment
with the hangman's hemp.

Confess no regrets, Gott im Himmel
knows I annihilated 10 million foes
for love of family, Fatherland
and the future human race. Consider
me an idealist for the Nazi cause.
Yet, I rue that dumb Arendt broad
described me as "terrifyingly normal,"
when I was so exceptional.

And I don't understand why
mein Führer gets so much attention
at Madame Tussauds just because
he grows a fine head of hair.
If only given the chance,
I could do better.

Rich as Croesus

They eat cake, fund wars and dance money away
as the sound resounds in our graveyards.

A once radiant sky turns murky. Voices
of angels mingle with the clamor of demons.

Valliant men and weeping women mourn
on snowy nights when music deserts mankind.

Only a silver voice, a rose in love, a bloody man
resonate as the countryside stares

with vacant eyes. The cynic looks backward
without pride and cannot look forward

with optimism. The words of prophets melt
off blank pages, pronounce there is no evil

where there is no man and there are no mistakes
in tomorrow. There is only the prospect

of willful denial like that of the ancient
Lydian king, so they may eat cake, fund wars

and dance money away while we drink laudanum,
bury our dead, scrape by and occupy nothing.

Water Music

Only those who frolic on the shore
are certain the trumpets precede love.

Water glides under a frenzied red, white and blue
sky while India ink flows from quill to score.

As the maestro streams his music
across the Thames to people, thirsting for life,

pleasure boats trace tunes written in water;
reeds, in unfathomed pain, follow wild wakes.

One traveler fears he does not belong,
another dreams with her eyes open to love.

Two on shore lay with bodies intertwined,
harboring secrets of their rhythm together.

In the distance, water and music
rise to join the voluptuous sky.

BEYOND ELECTRICITY STRANGE ENCOUNTERS & VISITS TO DYSTOPIA

Beyond Electricity

Stars shine through petite holes
punched in a velvet sky, waves
of magenta, yellow and cyan
showcase electric gardens
in prismed neon, plasma and LED
on Broadway while electromagnetic
languages ride photons racing through
tiny tunnels in ether to bring next day
newsflashes – all opera, conducted by man,
compositions from the Master of Electricity.

Silently abattoirs darken rivers brown,
out of the light, street jungles bleed
avenues crimson, fossils fuel excavators
that strip loam from mountain greenery
and black gold slowly propels us
back to stone and – no wonder – when
less than half-a-dozen electric stars slip
through the smog, tongues cease
and no electric gardens are lit – we wonder,
where is the master, the Master of Electricity.

Scherzo on *Blade Runner*
(reflexive poem)

Aardvarks and androids dream
of electric sheep in dystopia
Electric sheep dream of dystopia
Dystopia creates electric dreams
Electric dreams create dystopia
and dystopia creates a need
for the Master of Electricity
The Master of Electricity needs
sheep's dreams or there's no utopia
and no electric stars will be lit.

But electric stars will still be lit
because there's utopia in those dreams
the Master of Electricity needs
for the Master of Electricity
who needs dystopia to create a need
for the electric dreams that create
dystopia in electric dreams
of electric sheep in dystopia
who dream of the dystopia
in aardvark and android dreams.

Lost at Sea

When his ship crosses the Date Line
and gets trapped in a temporal loop,
Adam notices the day never changes.
Each morning, a Wednesday,
he decides to make the most
of his experience, learns to say
hello, goodbye and thank you
in the ship's 34 tongues.

He finds an ability to attend
shipboard activities simultaneously –
at two bells, he yoga-stretches, plays
Ping Pong and wine-tastes at three venues.
He savors a facial, massage and manicure
in three different salons at four bells
and at eight bells, sings piano-bar karaoke,
dances to the ballroom's Paradise Duo
and masters Sleight of Hand on deck.

Bored, terminal ennui drives him
to philosophy. To relieve this tedium,
he lugs Kierkegaard from the library
to his stateroom, learns temporal
orientation is the root cause.
When Wittgenstein tells him
language and symbols cannot
convey reality and Whitehead says
truth is always halfway there,
Adam turns to mathematics.

If he can reduce himself
to absolute zero, he can
divide himself into one and
become infinity, like god, he
may escape this temporal loop.

The next morning, a Wednesday,
when the steward opens Adam's
stateroom, he notices a single
Ping-Pong ball bouncing
back and forth off the walls.

The Tab

Knees, knuckles and fingers threatened,
Eric flees his flat, rivulets of sweat flowing
into rivers of fear, loan shark goons
in hot pursuit. Treed at a Eurostar station,
he remembers his father saying
a train travelling at the speed of light
can play tomorrow's songs and $E = mc^2$
so Eric commandeers a TGV to Paris,
hopes to rev it up beyond the speed of light
so he can either tear into tomorrow
or turn into pure energy and escape,
but Shylock's men jump aboard
just before he approaches warp speed.
Engine faltering and trapped,
Eric locks himself inside the cab.
Pursuers shatter the door, find
a gnat buzzing around the throttle,
humming top tunes of 2053.

Not a Cento Sonnet
on Reality and Truth

Even if you define a tail and trunk as legs, truth is
an elephant really doesn't have six limbs.
Though color-blind may say blue is black, it's not.
One's truth isn't always true and may not exist at all.

Sages say aardvarks and stars aren't real without us.
Actual things occurred Day 1 of the Cosmos,
but no one knew, since reality requires a mind
to define and might be an illusion like cinema.

Truth, you get mooned by emperors in invisible robes,
but actuality oft leaves much to imagination.
                              Yet, can man
bear too much Reality TV? Is action the sole proof of sex
and is there no truth,
              only our interpretation of scripture?

Truly, this is not really a truth and reality sonnet,
since one day both concepts
              may be proven non-existent.

Preparation for Travel

courtesy of the Prado Restaurant menu

With approaching Southwest 1899
noisome above the patio, we lade

Russian standard Moscow mules
ginger beer, vodka and fresh lime
juice follows Jameson's Irish mules
Dark 'N' Stormy bitters Meyers
also enhances ginger beer
Then Saint Archer draft
heads Red Trolley, flashing
green and ballasting, points to
Stella Artois Belgium
and Van Gogh Dutch
By the glass or pitcher
red, white, pink Sparkling Split
Grand Marnier Margaritas
Prickly Pear, Pomegranate
or Cointreau shaken tableside
Bellinis and Martinis
Peach, Pear, Mango
swim in gin or vodka
Blood orange blossoms
to the cranberry Cosmos and
we're gassed to go, but
don't ask our server
who's cook'n

Boxing and Logic

If tango is sex and chess together,
boxing is the tango on steroids.

Yet unlike chess, boxing's rule of thumb
defies logic like the game: *Rock-Paper-Scissors.*

Usually, an *out-fighter* floats like Ali,
stings like a bee to best a *brawler.*

The *brawler* may not dance well, yet sports
enough Herculean muscle to overcome an *in-fighter.*

The *in-fighter*, no Fred Astaire, produces power
and technique sufficient to wear down an *out-fighter.*

Except Ali defies the boxing rule and holds
the advantage over brawler Foreman
                              and in-fighter Frazier.

So it's hard to admit why my son
beats me in Scrabble, Cribbage and Gin.

The Chicken or the Egg Flarf

Scientists say the egg came
before the chicken, eggs
whether they evolved
to lizard, crocodile, platypus
or even our chicken,
predate the animal itself.

However, if you mean which came first,
the chicken egg or the chicken,
the answer is not as obvious,
even to scientists.

If the Red Jungle Fowl and the Grey
Jungle Fowl, the original proto-chickens,
got it on and laid
a Jungle Fowl egg that mutated to
the first chicken,
then the chicken came first.
If the Red or Grey Jungle Fowl got laid
and created an egg, with OV17 in it,
the compound found only in chicken eggs,
then obviously the chicken egg came first.

Bible-toting, pulpit-pounding propagators
of fundamentally wrong science,
such as flat earth and creationism,
disagree based on Genesis 1:20-21:
Let the skies be filled with birds of every kind.
So God created. . .every kind of bird.
No mention of eggs here.

Our conundrum continues in practical life:
Prize-winning economists can't agree
if supply-side or demand-side is better
for growing an economy,
sagacious political pundits can't agree
on guns or butter for growing the peace
and learned philosophers can't agree
whether art imitates life or life imitates art.

Cracker Animals

At the corner weed dispensary I buy a box
of psychedelic animal crackers and soon,

Rot and corruption termite our houses,
slime slugs slippery sidewalks.

Unprotected sex rabbits our ghettos,
but Planned Parenthood peoples prosperity.

Ponzi perpetrators vulture bank accounts,
but bluebirds rainbow our treasure pots.

While crows stalk cornfields,
farmers hawk their crops.

Even as terror rottweils nations,
companionship shepards happy 'hoods.

Though the ignorant wall discord,
still migrants coyote across the Rio Grande.

When war hawks desolate our fields,
peace efforts dove tranquil landscapes.

I must not featherweight, but finish the stash
and bravely bull ahead through my mental chaos.

I thought I was growing wings
— Denise Levertov

Modern Day Icarus Complex

Darkness surrounds my skin
and I don't know where I am
while absurd lacy veins sprout
from my shoulder blades into black,
orange and gold butterfly wings.

No longer earthbound and bored,
I desire to soar the church spires, admire
forests afire, but fear the sapphire seas
churning below until Zoloft, lithium
and Seroquel ease me back to Earth.

Plea for Rhythm and Breath

The ruby neon of liquor store signs,
sweet smell of weed and the siren call
of nowhere tempts, but a vision of better
explodes like a shrapnel star above.

With the myth of *holy profits* washed away,
we can navigate the dynasty of hell-fire
and bay of storms on a cloud cushion
over rusty pick-up trucks on crusty soil.

Clocks struggle blind and dumb with hands
broken, fingers numb, yet visions emerge
as we limit bobcats, diminish dinosaur fuels,
capture power from the wind and stars.

But we need to be fungi growing wise
in darkness, lest a sea of years evaporate
and the smell of grated ginger will linger
no longer as kitchens narrow and shut.

Master of fauna, flora and rock, give me voice
to air the language of rhythm and breath
for our children, so my plea spins beautiful
like a spider suspended in sun-sparkle.

Dies Irae

Who's Chernabog?
Only the most powerful villain Walt Disney ever created.
—Ridley Pearson

Children disco the checkered strobe-lit floors.
The specter of Chernabog mounts the bald pinnacle.

He sucks art, music and literature
from boulevards and graveyards .

Young minds sync thoughts with Milltown,
not Milton, Shakespeare or Keats.

Needle culture and chalk silhouettes
over pavement while street gangs, skulls
and bones thrust upward reeking red.

Babylon incites Blue Meanies, purple rain
stains idle brains and the hood stills
before sun-up, but minions return.

All our children have gone, every one after
Pied Piper penny-whistles vacant sounds.

Hieronymus Bosch paints empty words
on whitewashed walls. Norman Rockwell
grieves silently as he waits for Pelham 123.

Only prophets notice chestnuts fall from diseased trees
while Chernabog smiles and sees all is good, *very good.*

While Rachel cries, some learn relief comes
in the final breath. Other parents raise funds
to finance the piper's silence.

Passages

Rife with doors and gates, the universe
abides, as a full moon dwindles into nil,
breeze transforms to trees,
frost freezes fast on grass
and bright stars, laced in clouds,
pass over hillsides and dells.

Awakening to everything as an entrance,
I watch collies fly into fuchsia Frisbees,
boys soar into Japanese warrior kites
on Central Park green and see money
as a knife we plunge into each other,
like cords of wood loom as future pyres.

Chickens, pigeons and red hawks
may replace doves in the final days.
Ancient plowshares won't till
tumultuous earth, so I'll not wait
for a fireworks extravaganza,
but live for a trice of ice cream.

Trebuchet

Most Mondays, I'm up more or less sane,
as your voice, a viol through my pores, wafts
from its safe place, a cup of tea and jellyroll.
You note sea-salt shaken violence and horrors
of hateful hours blast our country's wardrobe.

Your story unfolds as I'm hit and run
by an errant golf cart like howling winds
and creaking oaks. Maybe the story
won't' happen, like winged gargoyles
taking flight, but nevertheless, I tremble.

I only wish fireflies could tango with stars
and we would waltz like snowflakes,
but I hear the swish of a scythe cutting wheat
below Van Gogh's crows, see train wheels
screeching to nil like holiday sparklers.

Red glare of expressway taillights at night,
chains and bridges of cigarette ash flash
through my home security system.
Boulders thrust through my castle walls
shake then shatter my sense of security.

Tyrannosaurus Wrecks

Accompanied by a steaming spot
of orange pekoe, I speak
raspberries and bran to her
blueberries and bananas.
As the breakfast sun glints
our kitchen glass, we feel
violent vibrations from the garden
as tyrannosaurus wrecks tomorrow.

The *Dystopia* Channel in the corner
broadcasts a grim fairy tale
with a giant orange ogre
who cannot suffer little children
and doesn't abide the chatter
of foreign matter. Waifs
and unarmed migrants roil
among flummoxed border guards
while venomous messenger pigeons
swoop in from fortified aeries above.
Terrified tots and toddlers scatter
to Chicago and points unknown
when a portcullis rises to release
them from their transparent fence.

In ogre-speak, we hear
Let's build a moat and wall
to settle it once and for all.
Raspberries and bananas
billow from our bowls.

The flute of the Pied Piper has never left us.
— Dimitris Mita

Campaign Promises *Par Excellence*

He roars over America on his golden wing. *Apostle*
and *Celebrity Apostle* broadcast his silver tunes.

He tootles glossolalia through his flute, Hispanics
hear Spanish, businessmen dollars and all others

their region's patois. The Piper promises
Star Trek force-field border fences and only

people with authorized chips in their ears
can beam through this invisible barrier.

Half of us will pay no taxes, all others, less
because the magnetic shield prevents cheap imports.

He rewrites regulations so our businesses mushroom.
Ford, Chrysler and GM each savor a 50% market share.

Our unfettered economic engine squeezes national debt
to zip and expands GNP so there's untold surplus.

Road repair assures jobs for all. Social Security
retirement age dips to 16 for those who opt out of work.

Neighborhoods, barrios and ghettos revert to Eden,
policed by blue knights and space-age drones

and America is safe abroad, protected by its high-tech
military and, at home, by the impenetrable border.

America prospers as the Piper whistles sounds
of soda water fountains and lemonade springs.

Revelation Today

Good grief, gods do what they like.
They call down hurricanes with a whisper
or send off a tsunami the way you would a love letter.

— Sappho

Man drives his black Mercedes fed
by carbon and sweat, joins a red Ram
running rampant in the Mid-East.

His silver BMW speeds crimson
highways of civil strife in Dallas,
Minnesota and San Bernardino.

I watch Hurricane Sandy submerge
New York and New Jersey, waters
and winds wash sand and souls away.

Travelling west past Virginia, see
miners crushed, streams sullied
and mountainsides stripped.

Rivers leap above aits and levees,
cascade over crops along the Ohio,
mighty Missouri and Mississippi.

I turn south at Kansas where
wheat stalks and sunflower thirst
in the blazing sun and wither.

Orange California cliffs crumble
into a Pacific rife with red tide
and empty fishing dinghies.

Oklahoma's locust-stripped fields
erode, shudder with each ounce
of water extracted from its bed,

The pale hearse of death
arrives, greeted by grooms
of greed and insouciance. . .
or maybe the gods
are just having fun
at our expense.

Super Blue Blood Moon

While I sleep
the moon plays tricks
silhouettes the cross
at Mount Soledad
and bewitches my bedroom walls
Fresh air rings the horizon
Black brown red yellow and white
hands interlock
form rainbows
across the countryside
throughout every city suburb and exurb
Farms and fields replace
bomb blasts
Guns melt and community gates –
no longer needed
Biology and geology
supplant superstition
The young volunteer
to nurture the landscape
and serve the poor
In Washington
civic duty trumps greed
Businesses aim service at all
The meaning of life
floats among the clouds

An empty trailer rattles
our well-rutted road
The super moon poofs
and a rising sun
shatters the spell

Wind Turbines Amok

Just past Morongo Casino,
a radio pundit blasts his shrill ill will,
telling me and all non-believers,
to be tolerant of intolerance and
intolerant of tolerance, as
my Audi zips eastward on I-10 over
the sand-brown San Gorgonio Pass
through a silver-metal army
of thirsty turbines, sucking wind
from an aqua sky as I pass by.

I overtake a few early sentinels
some idle at their posts, others
lazily spinning electricity. Midway
through this mechanical garrison,
where thousands of two- and
three-pronged props merrily whirl
to earn their keep, I'm uneasy,
sensing a freight-train-rumble.

As a rise pops up to my left, the radio
spews another typhoon-force huff –
extremism in defense of ideology is a virtue.
The turbines rotate so fast they almost melt.
SCROOSH, rotors lift a large swath of earth
50 feet up – a floating island with propellers.
I brake, countering hurricane-force winds
and warily watch this pseudo-spaceship soar,
wondering where roaring rhetoric
will take this flying arsenal of vitriol.

Tempest

Florence and her Sisters

The Wild West Show rambles on,
but this isn't her first rodeo
or trip over the concrete prairie.

A sea of broken glass
from out of bounds
pellets the shoreline.
Blind rose hips sip the sea
and struggle to hold sand
at their feet, the asphalt
garden ebbs and flows
to stem the roaring tide.
Stone fruit wither by
rocky lanes, trees torn
from turf, buildings strewn
like giant *Pick-up Sticks*
as she, in her fury, rages
at the burden from centuries
of neglect and abuse.

She offers organized chaos
for all swimming sea creatures,
but the mollusks hang steady
and we wonder why.

Don't Knock Hard Rocks

A politician denies effects of global warming,
says sea levels rise because rocks roll
into our oceans and his ignorance burns
credibility like a Nazi furnace renders hate.
Disenfranchised Palestinians hurl rocks
at soldiers who respond with knee-level
molten metal as self-interest trumps diplomacy.
Rock of Ages fail to cleft for students
or concertgoers as molten metal
from deranged shooters scatters all
from supposed sanctuaries.

That politico must have rocks in his head.
Rocks get a bad knock, why not praise
rocks for breakwaters, countertops,
walls and structures? And because
they often reveal fossilized ancestors,
filter water and pave roads. Our kids
can skip, climb and throw rocks.
We grind rocks for chalk pottery, pencils
and enjoy rock-salted wintry roads. Salt lick
keeps cattle happy while rock music keeps
listeners happy. In olden times, rock ballast
kept ships upright and castles tight.
Praise rocks, they're much better
than glass for building houses.

The Dark Knight Rises

CNN and my Yahoo home page
flow over the threshold,
seep under my bedroom door.
I see him sneak in:
face white with greasepaint,
red mouth appears slashed
to a *Black Dahlia* grin,
his traffic cone-orange hair
jutting from under a helmet,
a stare vacant as a school parking lot
at midnight.
Costumed in gas mask, armored vest,
leg and throat protectors,
his tactical gloves hold a Smith & Wesson
M&P 15 with hundred-round drum.
Faux-joker fires:
shhwaakkk   shhwaakkk   shhwaakkk.
Perfectly round blood puddles
spread on a waxed floor.

Suddenly, I am swept
into a Hobbesian nightmare
to the cusp of a Mad Max world-to-be:
zebras are braying Second Amendment rights,
535 penguins prate laws to require every
breathing soul regardless of criminal record,
mental stability or driver's license number
to own assault weapons,
666 junk radio pundits spew venom
promulgating a right to manufacture
WMD's in every basement
throughout America.

Hands tied, I'm in the National Gallery, Oslo,
viewing Munch's *Scream of Nature*.
It becomes a mirror.

Tally to date: San Ysidro 21, Killeen 22, Columbine 13,
Virginia Tech 32, Binghamton 13, Fort Hood 13,
Colorado 12, Newton 27, Washington Navy Yard 12,
Charleston 9, San Bernardino 14. . .

The Perfect Soldier

Land mines are my perfect soldiers.
　　　　　　　— *attributed to* Pol Pot

Hidden here below the sod,
I am the perfect soldier,
sentry and servant.
Once on my post,
I have no requirements,
my assigned territory secure.
Enter my space, I spring to action.
Fearless, I lie in wait 24/7,
never surrendering and ready
to sacrifice all for duty.

No matter who you are. . .another soldier,
an old peasant woman, a farmer,
three kids kicking a soccer ball
or just some dumb beast, my job –
neutralize you, remove you from battle
and tie up others to care for you.
I go by many handles,
Frog, Drum, Betel Leaf, Corncob,
all rightly non-pejorative, since
I am only a tool following orders.

After the battle is over
and the treaty ink dry,
obedient to my old commandants,
I rest in this peaceful field to eternity
or until I myself am disarmed.

At the Cambodian War Museum

Cat, once a man – a patch-quilt now –
body sculpted like Angkor Wat bas-relief,
tells of his 10 lives since age 11,
facing the Khmer Rouge and surviving
throughout the Cambodian War.

Meanwhile, a graveyard of Russian
and U.S. weaponry waits, mud-covered
in olive drab among flowering white trees,
fuchsia vines, glossy green-leaved bananas,
tropical humidity and sweltering tourists.

Cat's remaining body, the result
of a man-child forced to fight someone
else's war for survival rations, tells his story
better than world-renown inscriptions nearby,
each of his wounds, a life-shattering event.

The separate arm, chest, stomach, groin
and leg scars tell of five lives, but two
land-mine wounds overwhelm me –
the glass eye and prosthetic leg. Diabetes,
fever and concussions – afterthoughts.

At last he's ready to walk us through
the metallic graveyard of genocide,
yet it seems unnecessary to see or touch
the land mines, rifles and other U.S.
and Russian implements of man's cruelty.

A Soldier's Pain

homage to Brian Turner

Children frolic with you
in the concrete rubble,
an old man chats, offers chai.
Tomorrow they may gambol
over your fresh grave.

The swarthy arms dealer
beckons, a young son wriggling
in his arms, tells of blood shed
on the street. Yesterday, he sold
the RPG that'll kill you tomorrow.

No place is safe in Baghdad,
even lions and bears, escapees
from the zoo, may roam malls,
maul you or take your life,
if the IEDs don't.

Black body bags lie at your feet,
whisper silently to each other,
asking Allah why they died
in the bazaar blast and yet
you live another day.

Saffron sheets billow in the sun,
waiting on a dusty rooftop
for a mother to dress
her two youngsters, slaughtered
on the street this morning.

How fortunate we are
Allah, Yahweh or God
sets boundaries
on our imagination.

Morning: June 12, 2016

I wake and cannot believe, blood spurts
across the tile, the red clogs gutters
and gushes through my darkened door.
Shhwaakkk, shhwaakkk, shhwaakkk
to a Latin beat replaces drum, bass
and a joyful trumpet blare, confuses
three DJ's and the sans souci crowd
of dancers driven to the floor, piled on
each other like stampeding buffalo amid
smoke and streams of futile screams.
Mud of hate mixed with acrid blood
from a devil-seized mind flourishes below
disco balls and klieg lights. A reincarnation
of human terror and agony cast in Rodin's
Gates of Hell and depicted in Michelangelo's
Last Judgement on Sistine Chapel walls and
grotesque sections of Hieronymus Bosch's
Garden of Earthly Delights splatter
all over my white sheets and pillows.
Today, I see the pale horse of death
pulse beyond my pounding brain
and another 49 victims.

Morning: June 13, 2016

I wake and believe I'm Kafka's
giant beetle, helpless on my back,
realize my actions and those
of my friends cannot change lives
nearly so dramatically as a flood,
tornado or deranged gunman.

Better that I get out of bed, pick up
after my dog, cheerfully greet
strangers and neighbors alike
and eat my oatmeal and not stew
over the pits of domestic terror
or international disaster.

Though at times, I'd prefer to act
as Mother Teresa, I brew coffee,
clean gutters and help friends mulch.
Yet my humanity whispers,
Should I try to tip Quixotic cattle
or chase Alice's white rabbit down
the trail into its darkened warren?

CLOSER TO HOME

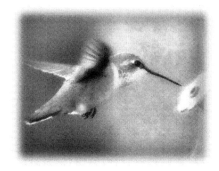

Dog Walking
homage to Kurt Brown

Neighborhood mornings, neighbors
take little or long walks to relieve
their dogs so those Tootsie Rolls
or puddles are not left in the kitchen
for mother to find. Sometimes dogs
wretch and try to re-eat the result,
but like us, they're family members
that eat, grow fat, guard the yard, sleep
and fart. Sometimes you have to stop
because they bolt across the street
to greet another Fido, Fifi or Xavier.
Other times, you have to fetch water
or play *fetch*. Dogs are always around,
dressed in their fur coats even during
the hottest days, expecting to be petted,
attended, asking for more chow, treats
and attention. Even when you make love,
they lurk, continue to have their wants
and needs. You get up in the morning,
comb what hair remains and suddenly
you're grooming him, removing
stubborn fur destined for your floors.
Listen to his bark, whimper, growl
or breath and watch his tail, he's
communicating *there're people at the door,
I'm starved, parched, upset or happy.*
Maybe that's what the Tootsie Rolls are for,
they're your dog's appreciation, just like
that lick of toe, hand or chin. Logic tells
my Roger how much I cherish his discard,

after all, he sees me follow and pick-up
after him with a transparent produce bag
or newspaper sleeve as he freely shares
his love. When his upward browns meet
my downward hazels, a transcendent nectar
flows the ether, binds our brains as one.

The Last Kiss

Dammit, you would ask me.
The only last kiss that moved me
came from our tri-color corgi.
How can I tell you about that when you
will tell of last kisses that overshadow
Juliet's famous farewell smack,
Rick and Ilsa's *au revoir* in *Casablanca,*
or Michael's death-kiss to Fredo in *Godfather II*?

I'm told good stories are authentic,
so here's my Truth or Dare tale:

Barely able to move, but certainly
able to pee all over the place, eyes
clouded milk white, Evan lies
on the vet's table, tube connected
to his vein. The sedative flows.
I feel him relax, become still,
as I cradle his head. My eyes blur.
There is one final lick on my hand
before he falls asleep, snores.
The vet looks at me; I nod.

Around Clairemont

8:30 a.m., San Diego 92117

Over the wall, a giant bonsai pine watches
14 Italian cypress line dance in the wind.

An orange tiger cat crouches on the stucco wall,
her windshield wiper tail sweeps left, right.

A lizard leaves his tail with the predator
like the eucalyptus shedding bark and leaves.

Twin grey Silverados nuzzle
in a neighbor's driveway.

A red hawk pirouettes over the canyon
with three crows in military pursuit.

Through fence slats, a green ribbon fern extends
long fingers like a dissident grasping for freedom.

Blinded cars kiss in anger, as boat and trailer
docked at street corner await the next tsunami.

On a high wire, three morning doves lament
as two motorists discover conflicting views.

The sun warms its way through the coastal layer
to see 14 Italian cypress at peace by the wall.

Ghost Gardening

homage to Kurt Brown

One in four of us plants tomatoes,
lettuce, greens, beans and such
for fun, food or both. These plants
grow, strive to live and have sex –
not quite like us, but nevertheless
they garnish our yards, planter boxes,
even abandoned porcelain toilets
and expect us to take care of them.
They require water and manure
plus pruning to save them from
their own unbridled fecundity.
They strut their fresh reds, maize,
greens and purples, need weeding,
and seek relief from pests and thirst
when I'd prefer a weekend
at the beach or in the mountains,
but I get up at dawn to brush
my teeth and instead grab
the cantankerous hose, sprinkle
ersatz rain, slay tobacco worms
and aphids, spray fungus and pull
crabgrass that goes on growing
stubborn like my mother-in-law.
Maybe in gratitude, plants
produce fruit and seeds
far beyond their needs
so we too may feed.

Listen and you may hear corn
growing – or in my garden,
the ghost of a child lost to suicide,
memorialized by the crepe myrtle
that centers my small vegetable patch.
I fear removing it and feel destined
to protect all flora. Yet, I dig out
old recipes, dig up the crops,
and appreciate ghostly garden gifts.

Hummingbird

Below my perch in the old cherry tree,
an emerald sheen and ruby red scarf
shimmer in the early summer sun,
wings flutter invisible as the sound
they make, while a needle syphon
penetrates a vamping flower.
Nature displays the beauty
of one hand washing the other.

Sound of Absence

I hear the dog breathe, the walls sigh.
Mirth and Joy disappear into the woodwork,
Peter Rabbit and Dr. Seuss retire to the bookshelf.
Kings, queens, jacks no longer at hand,
await the next war in the old desk drawer,
toys and games recover in the oak wood chest,
the land of counterpane rests in the linen closet.
Disney no longer omnipresent in the airwaves
is just part of the memory.
The house is quiet and the dog lonely.

The Bear and the Fish

Flush with cash
from the North Slope job,
Errol purchases a walrus tusk,
hires Ukluk to carve a scrimshaw bear,
returns week after week
only to hear: "Soon, soon."

At last "soon" arrives,
he gets a fish.
"How can this be?
I asked for a bear."
The Eskimo smiles and says
"I searched and searched your ivory,
but there was no bear at hand
only a fish trapped within."

When I start to write a verse or so,
thoughts hiss through pen,
ink flows into words.
Often a bear becomes a fish.

From out of the past come
the thundering hoof beats
of the great horse, Silver!
— from the radio intro

The Lone Ranger

From out of the west
into our 14-inch Motorola,
the Lone Ranger visited
us at 6:30 Sunday evening
along with Silver and Tonto.
We knew it was time
when our neighbor Caroline,
too old for dolls, young for boys,
galloped down Boulevard Drive
to join in the adventure.

Gun shot out of evildoer's hand,
lasso around the Cavendish gang,
fisticuffs without concussion
and other non-violent violence
rapt us to the rabbit-eared box.
Whether any story could be true
mattered not for we were captive
to *Kemo Sabe's* spell of justice
when we heard the *William Tell*.

Monday Night Football

San Diego

Was it worth going to the Jack Murphy?
Parking an issue, we leave the car
at Old Town and get vacuum-packed
into the trolley. Thirty-nine dollars
for food I would not feed my dog Roger,
so much noise I was glad
my hearing aid was at home
and finally the long lines
to another vacuum packed trolley ride,
this time at midnight. The next day I see
my son's *Facebook*. Throughout the U.S.,
all his friends see the pix, learn how
his Texans win on the last play
of the game in a fantastic comeback
and what a great time he had.

My mind goes back to a night in Atlanta.

An orange sunset eases the brutal summer heat,
cold-cut watermelon wafts in a slight breeze
as my dad and I walk to old Ponce de Leon park,
cross at the Sears traffic light and enter the din.

The Crackers play Birmingham, big deal tonight,
crisp green grass, taste of popcorn, front row seats
near our dugout, where aspiring minor leaguers
shake hands with young fans seeking autographs.

On a page torn from dad's notebook
I get Ted Cieslak and Lloyd Gearheart, heroes
to a boy of eight, great in Double A,
but couldn't cut it in the "Bigs."

Their names and feats lost in a cluttered past
until now as I look at my son's *Facebook* page,
how wonderful – going to Monday Night Football.

Up and Down the Florida Keys

Ninety-eight mile spine, along
aqua, green waters, corn silk
beaches, Bogart and Bacall's
Largo toward Hemingway's
Key West, Jimmy Buffet mood.

Courtyard palms shade
tiki bar flooding us en route
with spirits, Fish House
filling us with mariscos,
one platter after another.

Old town Key West, redolent
bougainvillea, Duval Street
venture, ancient drag Margo
at Bourbon Bar, swashbuckling
wreckers risking all in recovery.

White-frame Papa's house,
loft in back garage beneath
rising sun, source of stories
and lies beside six-toed felines,
above and below the surface.

Flashing blue in my rear view,
"Reason for 49 in 30 zone?"
"Stupidity, Sir." Honesty,
a $249 savings, but the story,
a blue sapphire heirloom.

Traffic

slows to a furlong per fortnight on the Five, like paddling a canoe in Jell-O. I wonder what bozo blocks progress of the little boy with flaxen hair in the adjacent Ford SUV who transports me back to childhood – no recall from my Cincinnati, Buffalo, Mendota, Ithaca days, other than tales told later and photos taken, but I clearly see Tullahoma, where red mud prevailed and I tossed my cookies in the back seat of our '38 Pontiac after eating boarding house stew with real chicken claws to suck on and thought the used-car lot was SantaClausLand because of red, white and blue pendants and light bulbs strung out front. Jacksonville, I jumped from a second story window to play with friends, was coerced into frolicking on stage as an almost nude Indian in a nursery school spectacular, ocean-swam by sandy beaches after travelling over a downtown trestle bridge and withstood the terror of the 1940's comic-book Hawkman soaring through my dark-cloud dreamscape. Macon, I learned not to shoot toy cannon pellets through the window of the model garage father built for my Christmas – it did not grow back or get replaced – lived in an abandoned gas station, pumps still outside, got scolded for playing in waste water with a black boy about my age. Atlanta brought other restrictions when I tested mother, not appreciative when I ruined a new leather jacket building a fort of abandoned tires behind a filling station, refused to wear my war-rationed sandals after boys in Mrs. Barnes' class laughed, crashed through a glass top coffee table, swiped candles from the church and told Pastor Kirkoff his fly was open while my mom schmoozed with him.

To teach me a lesson, maybe God told my father to chop heads off my Easter ducks and some older boys to sever the legs off a white puppy on streetcar tracks trembling in back of our house. The little boy moves on and I slowly creep past remains of two 18-wheelers, prone across three expressway lanes to be free at last.

A Christmas Eve Sonnet

Oak embers radiate cheer, bulbs
glow gold, red and blue while tinsel
silvers spiked greenery as snow piles
outside. Candy canes and gumdrops flavor
my favorite ornate branches, silver sounds
abound – mirth, joy and delight. Pine
turpentines the air while orange and clove
spice this earthly orb. A little Lionel
circles ribbon-wrapped presents
under our tree, while angels soar,
all above this festive fray.
Though December days may be gray,
whether he's imaginary or no,
Santa's spirit lights my night
every time I see this year's tree
even though I'm 60-, 70- or 83.

Ashen Apple

The ashen apple of these days.

— Denise Levertov

An abandoned orchard reeks of cider,
bronzed balls of fruit rot to their cores
on a pathway floor. While green weeds
strangle ancient footsteps, an eight-foot
tripod ladder – four rungs cracked, one missing –
pokes between barren trees with some leaves
withered crisp and a few rotten apples
hanging from strands like broken spider webs.

A well-used box truck, now grey and rusted,
wants for cargo. The driver-side door rests
in a junkyard over the rise and two tires
that remain are flat as Kansas. The once
festive two-story farmhouse with boarded
windows missing, shudders as winds whistle
through its frame. Dingy white clapboard
cries for paint, but no one lives there to care.

When I, bushed and sweating from a long trek
through other farms, barns and relics,
stumble into this tragedy of time,
the pain of progress strikes me hard
and I wonder which highway, bridge,
shopping mall or even metropolis
will soon rust on the crust of this earth
as an ashen apple of future days.

A Search for Meaning

When we are no longer able to change a situation –
we are challenged to change ourselves.

— Viktor E. Frankl

This Easter Sunday, April the first,
an Easter bunny, cottontail up
three doors down, middle of the avenue,
squashed, then another, mid-lane
one block later, again supine,
crow carrion, canyon coyote hors d'oeuvres
A cruel April Fools' joke, an omen,
blasphemy, name it? Doesn't matter –

Fact.
It is what it is.
Reality.

Fool's errand to assign meaning
and develop feeling, make more
of this red, white and gray splatter
than what covers the road.
Yet, thinking how precious life,
feeling unsettled and a little sad,
I realize those acts and emotions,
consistent with my conscience, trump
any mythology, cosmology or ideology,
so I bend down and bag the road kill.

An Eerie Evening

The terra cotta warrior wanders off
its stand. Chagall shakes on the wall,
dishes roll out of their racks while
our old house shudders in denial.

Rattled out of my bed, thinking
This must be the big one, I expect
Pacific Beach will rumble into the sea
and we'll have ocean front property.

But vigorous vibrations only shuffle
our household effects, there's no tilting
toward the canyon nor tsunami roar,
so I resume my sonorous snore.

The rattled rooms illume an eerie green, air
whispers from beyond the gate, fallow
footsteps follow. At our door, knocks whorled,
accompanied by voices from an alien world.

I wonder whether anchovies, garlic or the extra
onion piled on last evening's pizza doomed me
to gastro-insomnia when I hear knocks again
and open to a cadre of orange spacemen.

ATLANTA SPRING

Atlanta Spring

When I was a kid, spring meant chores:
feed, weed, dig, plant, prune,
lop, sap and scratches
while I wanted to play ball.

Now I open the tattered album
and faded phantoms of the past
flood my memory with a Monet
canvas of what can never return.

Our modest home lies up the rise,
I feel a vernal sun green zoysia grass.
In the warm air, stomatic dogwood
and azaleas parade pink and white.

Blue hydrangea and pink hibiscus
blossom in concerto.
Silk-flowered mimosa puffs stir
among lacy fern-like leaves.

Firethorns berry reddish-orange,
creamy gardenia whorls
scent dark green waxy leaves
and compete with the honeysuckle.

A Japanese cherry lifts pink arms skyward,
the lilac-flowered wisteria blossoms
and climbs to top the weathered old pine
where imagination tastes what is to come.

Lawn Glow

Dining room table clear, dishes dry
on a wooden rack, fading sun rays
creep below the rise. Birdsong
and moonrise signal time to grab
a Mason jar and capture cold fire.

Forget discord of Sunday confessions
or those summer music lessons,
we dodge skeeters, slide over slugs,
race our legs off, hour upon hour,
to fill our empty jars with light.

Night after night, we shadow fire
across the lawn 'til we're chased
off to bed. With playtime through
and lids loosed, most captives
rush into the oncoming Dixie dew.

Every creature carefully captured,
but not cataloged in a time we weren't
who we are now, only kids drinking
nature with no sense of where we fit
in the sky or what we were doing.

Now dawn, all fireflies are gone
from our lawn. Ken, Jan and Jane
have vanished to places unknown,
but their absence wafts around me
and yells out loud, *Look at my jar glow.*

Autographs

Clouds and a setting sun ease the swelter,
cold-cut watermelon wafts as a breeze
stirs the neighborhood when we walk
to old Ponce de Leon ballpark.
Crackers play Birmingham tonight,
we're front row near the home dugout
where aspiring minor-leaguers
tolerate young fans questing autographs.

On a page torn from Dad's notebook,
Ted Cieslak and Lloyd Gearheart,
icons of my youth, scribble their names
for posterity – a page now lost. Fame fades
like a comet when those great in Double A,
can't cut it in the "Bigs." Now they're
mostly forgotten, except when I retrieve
their stats and smiles from cyberspace.

Sweltering Summer Night

lightning bugs fill our yard,
a few skeeters seek their fill.
Mr. Wilcheck whacks weeds
behind a rusty woven wire
cattle fence suspended
between termite-infested
four by fours,
Atlanta Cracker baseball
blares from his Philco:
Lloyd Gearheart on third,
Ted Cieslak whacks the ball
through the sultry air,
grass smell mingles with wetness
from the approaching Dixie dew
and drifts through my open window.
Game over, too hot to sleep,
I listen to the crickets.

Trolley

Atlanta, circa 1943

Our flickering cyber-screen reveals
I'm wearing short pants and sport a buzz cut.

An olive green and yellow streetcar
grinds still at the corner brick beauty parlor,
beginning my adventure, I climb
two steps, insert the token with an "A"
cut out and reverse a cane bench,
comfortable as any granite pillow,
to face downtown. Humidity seals
my shirt to the yellow cane. I squeeze
a sash lock and lift the window
for some breeze. Our conductor clangs the bell,
rotates his rheostat and the pole sparks
on hot wires overhead. A whiff of ozone,
we're underway. Turning wheels squeal
like they're enjoying rough sex on the rails.
We bump and grind to center city,
where men doff their hats, women wear gloves
to shop at Rich's, chop suey's an exotic meal
and for 25 cents, Roy Rogers rides
across the Capitol screen.

Trackless trolleys and buses now rule
our streets and the Metro thunders
underground, Avengers or Jedi knights
replace Roy tearing across the cinema
and exotic meals come in many tongues –
just as if we're in Babel – and yet I
still hear the clang, smell ozone
and feel a clickity-clack over rails,
thrilled to be in the only Atlanta I know.

When Making Date Nut Bread

I return to Atlanta in the 1940's.

The morning sun filters through the gauze curtains over the sink to highlight the stove in a kitchen built for only one cook.

Opening the recipe file, I see my mother.

So thin you almost miss her; a Roman nose, hair tightly coiffured and an olive complexion, she wears a blue-flowered white apron.

I take out a recipe card worn so thin, you can almost see through to your fingerprints.

She pulls a recipe card from the red and white diamond-patterned metal box, smiles and gathers the fixings.

While reading the card, I always note the rare typo, "nutes" spelled with an added "e."

The clackity-clack, messy ribbon and stiff keys of the old Royal surely caused the error.

I gather the ingredients and loaf pans, flood the dates, sugar, butter with boiling water, add the eggs, feather in the flour mixture and the "nutes."

Everything precisely laid out and in order, she mixes the ingredients.

I spoon into loaf pans, remove excess batter on the spatula and bowl with an expectant tongue
                                        of so long ago.

She finishes, calls and I run into the kitchen for a taste of the remaining batter while she places the loaf pans in the oven.

Soon warmth and comfort will flood the house.

The Dishwasher

As I bring dishes into the kitchen,
she is already running hot water
into the single sink and dissolving
powdered *Rinso* soap from its green box.

She takes the plates and carefully scrapes
our scraps onto yesterday's *Journal*,
slips on her yellow rubber gloves and starts
to scour every last bacterium
and virus into oblivion.
I stand at her right as she rinses cups,
saucers, plates and passes them to me.
With a thin white dishtowel, I wipe
and stack at parade rest in a wooden rack.

Whether the task was
nurturing us with the aroma
of apple, cinnamon, nutmeg,
or protecting us through the
role of dishwasher, it is so clear
my sister and I cocooned
within her armored bubble
until metamorphosis.

My Father's Slide Rule

rests on the oak wood desk,
in its tan leather sleeve,
his name neatly inked
on its weathered surface,
a red Pickett etched
on the working face,
no longer calculating
stress for a freeway bridge,
cubic feet of asphalt
for an airport apron
or slope for sewer line.

Demoted to memorabilia's
dumpster a half century ago,
its logarithmic scale is
still useful as a reminder,

hours drag in the teens,
increasingly speed up
twenties through the nineties.
By 60, they're traveling so fast,
you wish there were a time-cop
to stop and give them a ticket,
a welcome pearl for me – more time
to be less busy about my beans.

My Pond in Colorado & Along the Way

My Pond

High in the Rockies, far beyond noise,
my pond nestles between Quandary
and Red Mountain, silent sheen bordered
by spruce and pine leaning over to reflect
on her surface. Squirrels, fox, chipmunks
scurry about and an occasional moose visits
while feathered gray jays, red-tailed hawks
and copper condors soar above and trout
glide in weed forests and under fouled firkins,
waiting for a random dragons to skim above.
Sometimes wind-ruffled or frozen white,
she always returns to serenity.

Those secluded forests and critters
above and below continue their reveries,
while I return to city grays, perpetual motion
hustle on corridors of commerce
and the tension of verbal garrotes.
Yet I hear her calm and whisper across
mountain peaks, rivulets and plains,
always telling me to be still, endure.

On the Redwoods Trail

A tribe of redwoods stands huddled together
800 footfalls down, reaching for the skies.
Needles thin as vermicelli soak up rare sun,
tannin-laced sap guards families against intruder.
Tightly bonded groups often share a single seed,
individuals whisper *I've got your back*
when threatened by flashing and whistling furors.

Halfway down, we pass the highest treetops.
Trail end – those tops vanish to infinity
when we bend backward at the boles,
seeking a full view of Earth's tallest trees.

On the return climb, stepping over
the same banana slugs and tree roots
that impeded the trek down, our slow motion
is too fast and my obstructed heart screams
from below my son's sunburned face,
now washed white, and caring blue eyes
I'd never seen nor will ever forget.

Mountain Reflection

Somehow we strayed off Dicey's Mill trail;
wrong turn at Blueberry junction, I think.

Lost in the piney woods of Mount Whiteface,
Dave and I gather green wood for a fire
and hope, but the temperature plummets,
winds rise; the New Hampshire sky darkens.

A wetter than water mist
whistles through our ponchos.

Quivering, we manage an anemic fire,
feel a bit of warmth and set up camp.
Then the northwest wind wells
and the mist becomes a freezing rain.

We eat our dry food,
which tastes like mothballs,
climb into light sleeping bags
and belch camphor.

The ground turns to frozen stone.
We flee our flimsy cocoons, seeking warmth,
almost stand in the flagging fire,
scorch our jackets and melt
the rubber soles of our boots.

Many mountains later,
I stand on Blueberry Ledge.

A lone eagle performs the missing man
maneuver as it soars over the valley.

I reflect on that wretched night
and our shared laughs over 40 years.

Fort Stockton, Texas

The Texas sun melts purple and red
Crayolas into the side window ledge
of our '72 faux walnut and cream
Ford station wagon, Boo Berrys reek
from the box and Count Chocula spreads
all over the ersatz leather seats.
The man has been hanged, 20 questions asked,
alphabet repeated many times, names guessed
and the three boys tire of tormenting
each other and start whining *I'm hungry,*
Jason hit me, Andrew farted,
I need to pee, as we near Fort Stockton.
Wife glares and mutters,
I told you we should fly.

Passing a thermometer frozen
at 108 degrees, the boys spot
the Sonic drive-in on West Dickinson.
I surrender juicy T-bone steak dreams,
drive across the glaring white boulevard,
pull into a covered parking stall.
Hoping *Service with the speed of sound*
is no empty claim, I yell our order
for several corn dogs, burgers,
cheddar peppers, hand-battered onion rings,
cherry-limeade and chocolate soft serve
into the intercom. I pray for roller skates
at sonic speed, peace in the back seat
and elsewhere.

Parade

San Antonio

Six years old, he sits on the curb
in front of the Alamo, watches
the Battle of Flowers parade.
Precision R.O.T.C. units strut,
scouts carry U.S., Texan, Mexican,
multi-color fluttering flags,
followed by flowered floats.
Horse-riding señors and señoritas,
marching bands and bugle corps
blaring martial music,
colorful costumes and dresses,
antique Fords and Chevys honking,
giant helium balloons shaped
like caterpillars, tigers and stars
go on and on down South Alamo Street.

A red-nosed circus clown
with orange hair,
wearing a flower-covered
puffy white costume
comes over to offer candy.
From my son's expression,
I think he is having the time of his life.

Andrew stares, mouth wide-open:
Wow, what a great parade,
now a big caterpillar balloon
and a tiger one too. Wait, what's
coming next? Oh, oh. A big white-faced man
with a red nose, huge mouth, yellow teeth,
orange hair in a white sack
with big spots all over it,
and big shoes stomping the pavement.
What's that in his hand?
What's he going to do to me?
He's coming over to get me.

"DADDY"

Big Horn Medicine Wheel

We snake up Highway 14A
to the cutoff road, one-lane,
no shoulder, thousand foot
drop-offs either side, like a spine
connecting the Medicine Wheel
to the body of mankind.
Noisy boys quiet, then I hear
Watch the side, you're too close,
What if we meet a car? I'm scared.
When we get to the chain link
surrounding the sacred circle,
there's an old Lakota Sioux
at the nearest cairn,
sitting with his blanket full
of assorted promises.
A threadbare sombrero covers
his eyes, jeans and shirt drape,
and crags in his face are leathered
like weathered granite standing
in the neglect of time. I presume
booze hidden under the blanket.
As three boys run the perimeter,
expelling 400 miles
of backseat ennui, I examine
the stones arrayed in 28 spokes.
Aloud, I wonder *Why this circle?*
The old Sioux stands, strides over
and speaks soberly,

For 6,000 years, we come to this place
where ancestors built the sacred hoop
that shows mankind is forever bound
to his neighbor, to the land
and the great unknown. I fear
these ties loosening, the great
circle destroyed.
I sense imprinted in his eyes
the fear my boys faced
passing over the narrow spine.

Crawford, Nebraska

When the noon siren sounds,
strangers are shocked off their stools
while Wayne Lee and Amy P. chuckle.
Yet, if that danged siren sounds at 5:42,
a grim-faced Wayne and Amy
switch off *The Weather Channel*
or stop showing properties
and scramble to a nearby storm cellar.

Driving the Fossil Highway
just outside Crawford,
towards the bison bone bed,
we stop for a bite at Drifter's Cookshack.
Amy and Wayne say the food's great,
but don't eat the stuffed pheasant
(or other decor), so we drive on up
to the chinked log dinosaur.

Past empty saddles on the hitching post,
rustic wagon wheels and well-weathered
ten-gallon milk cans on the front porch,
we enter through a flapping screen door
to discover quite the menagerie of moose
and deer racks, red railroad lanterns, bear
bells, jugs and jars, horse collars and straps,
dusty pictures and plaques of recognition.

Passing the pot-bellied trash burner,
I jump back when a stuffed bison
appears half-in/half-out the shack.
Cannot help wondering if Bill Cody
chased the beast through the wall on his way
to visit Calamity Jane's tent and the gals.

I recommend the buffalo roast and combo grill.
Amy and Wayne would steer you to the rib-eye
with a side of cowboy beans
or the fire-grilled salmon
with the fried cabbage and apple side.
All of us agree on the sarsaparilla soda
and finishing with the homemade
apple pie; that is, unless you hear
that danged siren sounding at 5:42.

Lubbock, Texas

Bye, bye Miss American Pie

— Don McLean

Twenty years after
the morning the music died,
my mind wanders back
to that long, long ago –
when my youth is ending
and I'm about to face life.

It's 1979,
I'm in front of Buddy Holly,
at 8th Avenue, east of Q.
Buddy, all 8-1/2 feet
cast in bronze,
narrow lapels and tie,
stove pipe pant legs,
knees slightly bent,
Fender Stratocaster in hand,
frets still intact, looks down
from his pedestal at me
through those horn-rims.

Together, he and I joined
a cadre marching through
a window of history –
too young for War II, we gained
knowledge from the '30s
and were coming of age in time
for the post war expansion – until
his window slammed shut, shade drawn.

My window stayed open –
too young for the blood of Korea,
too lucky for the missiles of Cuba,
too old for the slaughter of Viet Nam,
my books were still open
inside ivied walls
that early morning
when the music died,

commercial concepts
absorbed my mind
inside the sandstone quad,
when John was taken,

Fanta advertising
captivated my brain
while Martin
preached his last

and my pregnant wife
occupied my thoughts as I drove
to Oregon and the radio cried,
Bobby died.

Why did my mine stay open
when so many windows
slammed shut? Like Jack Flash,
the years have passed
and if I ever know why,
that'll be the day I die.

I've Got the Bone Marrow Blues

Mississippi Delta

My doctor done told me
"A procto-exam ain't
a worrisome thing
that'll give you the blues
if I'm in a good groove
and you don't move."

My doctor done told me
in his cheerful way,
"You've got cancer,
but don'tcha fret, it'll grow
so slow, your heart'll be
the first thingamajig to go."

My doctor done told me,
a bone marrow biopsy's
in store, yells out the room,
"BONITA, if you please."
Expecting a pretty nurse,
it's an unwanted surprise,

BONITA's no lass, she's justa
Big Old Needle In The Ass.
I've got the bone marrow blues,
I've got the bone marrow blues.
Yeah, yeah, it's no wonder I've got
these low-down bone marrow blues.

My doctor done told me,
"I 've got bad news from the lab,
your marrow eats the baby reds
and whites won't share the sera –
but don'tcha worry, we'll fix you up
with a good dose of rituximab."

I've got the bone marrow blues,
I've got the bone marrow blues.
Yeah, yeah, it's no wonder I've got
these low-down bone marrow blues.

About the Illustrators

Author, illustrator, and watercolor artist, **LINDA S. NAGY** was born in Atlanta, and holds BFA and MFA degrees from the University of Georgia. She first worked as an illustrator for Hallmark Cards in Kansas City. She and her husband, Bernie, have collaborated on several award-winning regional Colorado coffee table photo books. The revised and updated third edition of *Rocky Mountain Wildflowers Field Guide* (High Country Artworks: 2019) is a pocket-sized book, intended for use while backpacking. A member of the Colorado Native Plant Society, she earned a Colorado Flora Certificate and Native Plant Master Certification.

BERNIE NAGY is a photographer, author and illustrator from South Park, Colorado.. Retired from a mail order/retail business, his first photo book received seven awards, including Best International Travel Book and Best illustrated Regional Travel Essay book. In 2012, he published *South Park Colorado Nature's Paradise*, also a winner of several awards. His second edition of *Rocky Mountain Wildflowers Field Guide*, created with his wife, Linda, received four awards. A correspondent and photographer for Colorado newspapers and magazines, he serves on the board of directors for the South Park City Museum in Fairplay.

CHRIS VANNOY served as the U.S. National Beat Poet Laureate (2017-19). His poetry has earned the San Diego Book Award four times: in 2007 for *Twenty Poems Against Love and A Song for The Air* (co-authored by Gabriela Anaya Valdepeña), in 2014 for *A Strange Summer*, in 2017 for *The Rest of It,* and in 2018 for *All There Is.*

162

ABOUT THE POET

JAY M. MOWER grew up in Atlanta in the 1940s and '50s. As an advertising and marketing executive, management consult, and advertising professor, he counseled companies and molded advertising professionals. Now retired in San Diego, he hung up that old blue pin-stripe suit and began writing poems.

He first started writing poetry while volunteering as a mental health facilitator. With more than 40 poems published in various journals and anthologies, he has compiled three chapbooks and has been a featured poet at readings in San Diego.

A graduate of Harvard (cum laude), he earned an MBA from Stanford. Jay is married, with three grown sons and three grandchildren.

The Eskimo carver selects a walrus tusk
begins to fashion a scrimshaw whale
but as he finishes, a polar bear
emerges from the ivory.

A man plans his career
begins on the road of commerce
before realizing a poet dwells
within his pin-stripe suit.

When I start a poem
thoughts hiss through my pen,
ink flows into words, but
my whale often emerges a bear.

Never wrote a poem, planned to write a poem or even read much poetry until a few years ago. Of course, I read some of the obligatory schoolwork poems – *Friends Romans Countrymen. . ., Frost on the Punkin, Mending Wall, Prufrock, et alia* – but had little interest in poetry beyond that until I facilitated Family and Friends support groups for the San Diego Depression and Bipolar Support Alliance of San Diego. For a while I just observed, but soon I felt a need to express myself as I heard many different voices coming from different places. Some shared pain, anxiety, grief, guilt, but sometimes humor and joy. I coupled these voices with my own which is influenced by our experience with a bipolar son. Fortunately, he successfully manages his disorder.

A poet member of the support group became aware of my fledgling efforts and invited me to read some poems at open mike poetry venues and my interest grew. I attended local workshops and even took courses at Grossmont College to learn more about techniques others use. Finally, I honed my skills enough to get a few poems published although my rejection rate was substantial at the beginning and remains high even now.

Since poetry is somewhat of a poverty profession unless you go into advertising, I write primarily for my own self-expression and share poems if I think others will enjoy them. Although my first poems dealt with mental illness, I do not write many poems about that topic today. As you paged through this volume you would have come across poems of love, concern about our society and environment, memoirs of travels, and some which are just plain ridiculous because the spirit moved me.

I do have an advertising and marketing background, which may be why there is not a consistent or single voice in my poems. I tend to write in a style to conform to the topic covered. Poems about relationships are written in straightforward and lyrical (I hope) style. Poems about the environment, politics or dystopia may be more symbolic. In most of my work you will find some irony and a second or third meaning if you look beyond the basic words.

In addition to getting prompts from memory like the *Atlanta* poems, or listening to people, as with the *Different Voices* poems, I use techniques that work for me. Sometimes, I will get a prompt from art or photography (ekphrastic poems), like those printed in *Summation*. Some of my poems were written to stimuli from workshops. More complex poems such as *Dear Clementia* had their origin in class assignments at Grossmont College. One poem, *Swamp Witch*, began with an offhand remark by playwright friend Cary Bynum, when he bemoaned that he enjoyed his trip to Houston save for the "bad gumbo" he ate.

Often a poem will more or less write itself. More likely I will do research and compile disparate ideas on a paper and use a process used in advertising, *mind-mapping*, to link concepts together and write from the grid I create. I also find some poems just sit in an unfinished pile for a while, then something will happen to draw me back and I will be able to complete them. There is always the poem that comes in a dream where ideas have been roiling – or should I say gestating – quite a while, and, of course, the ever-present rewrite like the poem than begins this Afterword.

This is my first volume of poems. I have created three chapbooks: *Light Medium Dark, Different Voices* and *Along the Way*. Some poems from them make up part of this collection.

As mentioned previously, since poetry does not wield great riches, I have to be satisfied in writing for myself; however, it is my goal in this volume to entertain, inform and challenge you, my readers, to appreciate poetry. As a consequence, most of my poems are written to be understood. Only once in a while do I write "language" poems, and when I do, look for a little humor. Even in the most obscure poems, I try to maintain some logical thread.

Enjoy.

JAY M. MOWER

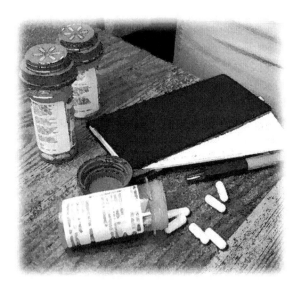

Acknowledgements

Some poems in this collection first appeared in these publications:

Acorn Review
Chaparral
Muddy River Poetry Review
Diaphanous
Summation (VI - X)
A Year in Ink
BEAT-itude Anthology 2018
Local Gems Halloween Newsletter 2018,
Magee Park Poets Anthology
San Diego Poetry Annual

Credits

Cover and Frontispiece
Poet in a Pin-stripe Suit
photograph by LINDA S. NAGY

Poet
Back Cover and page 163: LINDA S. NAGY

Interior Art

The Swamp Witch: BERNIE NAGY	p. 3
Monet's Bridge: JAY M. MOWER	p. 11
Boxing and Logic: CHRIS VANNOY	p. 17
The Blue Dancer of Buenos Aires: CHRIS VANNOY	p. 23
Different Voices: CHRIS VANNOY	p. 45
Joie de Vivre: BERNIE NAGY	p. 69
Rising Super Moon: BERNIE NAGY	p. 87
Hummingbird Feeding: LINDA S. NAGY	p. 119
Morning Reflection: BERNIE NAGY	p. 137
My Pond: JAY M. MOWER	p. 147
Hummingbird: LINDA S. NAGY	p. 162
Medicine: BERNIE NAGY	p. 166

Made in the USA
San Bernardino, CA
25 May 2020

72316402R00098